EFFECTIVE
WEBSITES
for
CPAs

Effective Websites for CPAs: Grow Your Practice and Profits
©2006 Kristi Stangeland

RJ Thompson Publishing
445 Hamilton Avenue
Suite 1102
White Plains, NY 10601

914.478.8480
www.rjthompsonpublishing.com

Cover design: Kathi Dunn, Dunn + Associates Design
Interior design & typesetting: Liz Tufte, Folio Bookworks

ISBN: 0-9779907-5-3
ISBN-13: 978-0-9779907-5-7

EFFECTIVE WEBSITES

for

CPAs

Grow Your Practice and Profits

KRISTI STANGELAND, CPA

Acknowledgements

Just as information travels at the speed of light through the information superhighway, this book has traveled around the world on my laptop over the course of six months. It started on a flight from New York to Luxembourg and ended on a flight from Fort Lauderdale to New York. Unfortunately, it did not move at the same speed as the Internet!

Writing can be a very solitary activity, but I feel blessed that I did not have to go down this road alone. I have many to thank for their helpfulness, encouragement and attentiveness during the time this book was in progress. I'm certain that I have left someone off this list, so I ask for forgiveness ahead of time!

First, I must thank my three favorite accountants: Peter Hinman (my husband), Betty Stangeland (my mom) and Sig Stangeland (my dad). Yes, I have been surrounded by accountants my entire life!

A number of people provided valuable input during this process. Many thanks to the following: Karon Thackston, Cindy Penchina and Bryan Eisenberg.

I want to thank all of my clients. I've learned so much from them over the years. I appreciate and greatly value their business! I would like to specifically thank my CPA clients for their feedback as I was writing this book. I offer my sincere gratitude to Dennis Kremer of William Greene, LLP; Steve Lamos of Lambrides, Lamos and Moulthrop, LLP; Mark Mottel of Mottel and Kluge, LLC; Donald Kluge of Mottel and Kluge, LLC, and Elizabeth Brown, CPA.

There aren't enough words to express my feelings for family and friends who eagerly shared my excitement for this project. Thank you for understanding when I was running late (or when dinner was running late). A special thanks to my children, Erika and Tina, without whom my life simply would not be complete, and to my in-laws, Clyde and Evelyn Hinman.

Finally, I would not be writing this book if it were not for John Eggen, Coach Rob, and Jill Clair from Mission Publishing, Yolande Korsten of ShadowRain Design, Meredith Kimbell from Corporate Adventure, Liz Tufte of Folio Bookworks, Devin GawneMark and Hobie and Kathi Dunn from Dunn+Associates. Thanks for all the resources and coaching!

Contents

Introduction

I was once told that a single issue of the *New York Times* includes more information than a person living in the 17th century would learn over his or her lifetime. Can you imagine? We take the availability of knowledge for granted because we live in such exciting times. Technology is expanding due to this knowledge and is quickly revolutionizing the way we do everything. As a CPA, web designer and Internet marketer, I've been watching this technology revolution up close and personal with great interest.

I believe the client development area of the CPA profession will be greatly impacted by the changes in knowledge and technology that are occurring today. I wrote this book to help CPA professionals understand and implement much of the technology made available through web design and the Internet. More importantly, I wrote this book to help you benefit from them. I've had many CPA clients develop web sites only because they felt they *had to* in order to keep the pace. They honestly had no great expectations about their site. But that all changed once they acquired their first new client through the Internet. Through the information and worksheets contained in this book, you'll be guided through a step-by-step process. When you've compiled all the details, you'll be well equipped to work with a web designer to create a site that meets all your goals.

In addition, this book is to educate. The Internet may seem confusing with all the hype and myths floating around. People hear terms like "organic search," "pay-per-click advertising" and "blogs," but don't have the time to investigate all these different areas of Internet and search engine marketing. This book will shine a light on these mysterious terms and also guide you in making the best decisions about your site and the marketing of it. You'll gain an understanding of the different ways your website can positively impact your business, what strategies may not be successful and what types of things to stay far away from.

Lastly, you'll discover the core reason for building and promoting your site: converting leads into clients. By eliminating many of the non-billable hours involved in lead generation, you'll see firsthand how your website can attract new business for your firm. The end result? A site that is functional, attractive and that represents your firm with the utmost professionalism.

1

The Internet Effect

"All great change in business has come from
outside the firm, not from inside."
Peter F. Drucker
U.S. Management Consultant

Do you remember what it was like 10 years ago before the Internet had become a way of business and life? Sometimes we become so entrenched in our professional schedules that we are oblivious to the changes around us. Individuals are becoming more isolated and self-sufficient as a result of technology. Over the past decade we have decreased the use of live bank tellers in favor of ATMs. We have begun listening to music through "Pods" with headphones rather than as a group with entertainment centers and speakers. We purchase airline tickets on our own via web portals rather than communicating with travel agents. The Internet has increased our isolation. We now order books online via Amazon.com rather than meandering through our local bookstores. We find goods and services through a Google search, then shop at midnight in our bathrobe rather than brave a crowded Wal-Mart store filled with swarms of people.

In 2004, Yahoo!, Inc. and OMD conducted an Internet Deprivation Study to examine consumers' media habits and emotional connection towards the Internet. Participants were asked to stop using the Internet for two weeks. All participants in the study experienced withdrawal and feelings of loss, frustration and disconnectedness when cut off from the online world. Users forced to remove themselves from online life struggled with their loss of convenient access to routine information like emails, banking transactions, bill paying, account balances and maps. In addition, and more importantly, lack of communication figured most prominently in the withdrawal process. Why? Could communication through the web be valued that highly? Yes!

The Internet gave people the ability to overcome time and distance barriers. They could create an effortless community where they could correspond at their own pace and within their own schedules via chat rooms, instant messaging, email and more.

One of the more amazing parts of the study: Yahoo! paid individuals $1,000 to participate. However, Yahoo! had a very hard time even getting people to agree to participate in this experiment. "This study is entirely indicative of the myriad of ways that the Internet, in just ten short years of mainstream consumer consumption, has irrevocably changed the daily lives of consumers. This is true to the extent that it was incredibly difficult to recruit participants for this study, as people weren't willing to be without the Internet for two weeks," said Wendy Harris Millard, chief sales officer, Yahoo!. That speaks volumes.

The Effect on Your Firm

Are you wondering what this has to do with your business? Who cares that individuals are becoming so dependent upon the Internet? Accounting has nothing to do with consumer behavior (webbased or otherwise).

That's a common misconception. And a deadly one. Behind every business is a group of individuals. If people have started using Switchboard.com to obtain phone numbers, Google for the latest news and MapQuest for directions, it is obvious that the channels of communication are changing. Phone books, newspapers and large, paper maps bought at service stations are going the way of the Model T Ford. (In fact, full-service gas stations in and of themselves have already practically fallen extinct.) Accounting firms that take notice of these changes will be in a more advantageous position to grow their practices and increase their profitability.

The Top Shifts That Affect Your Firm

Technology is changing people and their expectations. Including their expectations of your organization. As I see it, the top trends that affect you and your firm include the following:

Information Availability & Empowerment: Probably the greatest impact the Internet has had on everyone is in the form of information. It wasn't coined "The Information Superhighway" for nothing! Anyone who has a computer and an Internet connection can research and find out about the most obscure subject matter.

Wal-Mart, currently the nation's largest retailer, is known to intimidate both its suppliers and competitors. According to a *New York Times* article, Wal-Mart is starting to get nervous about Google because it is concerned that Google might soon be able to tell Wal-Mart shoppers if better bargains are available nearby. They are aware of the changes in consumer behavior and of the impact that it may have on their stores in the future.

Traditional professions, whose knowledge was rarely questioned, such as accountants, lawyers and doctors, are now coming under fire more frequently about their practices. Because of the enormous amount of information online, people in general have become more attuned to topics they never gave much thought to previously. Rather than simply taking someone's opinion about a disputed matter, an Internet-enabled person can easily do a Google search to find specifics about any topic. This instills an unofficial system of checks and balances that did not exist before.

These facts cause previously untouched professions (such as yours) to check and double-check everything they do in order to retain their credibility and authority. As if having the Financial Accounting Standards Board (FASB), the IRS and your local state breathing down your neck wasn't enough, now you get the distinct pleasure of defending yourself and your decisions to anyone who chooses to challenge you based on what s/he recently received in an email last week from Aunt Martha.

Loss of Loyalty: Did you know that in November 2005 actor Tom Cruise replaced his publicist, Lee Anne DeVette (who also happens to be his sister), with a veteran Hollywood public relations person? Who cares, right? However, a *New York Times* article reported that the biggest reason for the change was that Cruise was nervous. Why? The pool of bankable movie stars is shrinking. In a quote from the article, Allan Mayer, managing director at Sitrick and Company, a public relations firm, said, "The entertainment media is changing. The currency a movie star had was the ability to put people in the seats. They command enormous salaries. But simply having a star in a movie isn't enough. Young audiences don't have the same loyalties and interest that previous generations have. That's why there is so much panic in the industry." To keep his face out front and to keep himself well represented before a wider age group, Cruise dumped his own sister in favor of a larger firm.

OK, so you're not a movie star, you're a CPA. The same struggles with loyalty are yours, too. People are becoming more and more discerning and less loyal every day. In fact, a study conducted by Weber State University in 2002 by H. Lon Addams, PhD and Anthony Allred, PhD cited a wide range of reasons clients of CPA firms would consider leaving. A lack of pro-activity on the part of the CPA firm was the #1 reason followed by a lack of effective communication.

Sitting back and hoping for client loyalty is not a good strategy. It's time you make a move to earn their loyalty. Fortunately, this can easily be achieved with the Internet, when you are open to certain changes in the way that you currently do things.

It may seem like a bleak picture, but it isn't. The technology that is changing your clients' behaviors can easily be used by you to counteract the negative impact it may have on your firm. These are very exciting times with changes in technology occurring almost daily.

I have to assume you are ready to make these positive changes, or you wouldn't have bought this book. Some things you'll learn about with regard to web site design will be exciting. Some may be scary. All will lead you to a new way of providing exceptional services for your clients and offering a higher level of communication. With your new web site, you'll have the tools to increase client loyalty as well as reinforce your standing as a reliable authority that can be trusted and depended upon. You'll also be able to:

- decrease the length of your sales cycle
- keep clients abreast of changes
- increase sales of services
- generate more qualified leads for your firm
- provide valid information
- increase client retention
- and more

In order to guide you through the steps of creating (or overseeing the creation of) your site, we'll need to start with the basics. As we go through each step, you'll begin to see how they all play off one another. Each has its place and purpose in the process. So, let's get ready to dissect the aspects of an effective web site. When we're done, you'll know precisely what to ask your web designer to do and not to do in order to have a site that performs at maximum capacity to reach your goals.

2

The Real Value of Your Website

"Price is what you pay. Value is what you get."
Warren Buffet
U.S. Entrepreneur

Why have you purchased this book? What, exactly, do you want your web site to do? Do you have a vision for your Internet presence? Web sites can be very powerful additions to your practice, if they are built, maintained and marketed properly. They can also be a colossal waste of time, money and energy if they aren't. Before you get too far along in the process, give that question some thought. Let's take it one step further. Write down your goals for your web site on the next page.

Goals for My Web Site

I want my company's web site to:

1. _____

2. _____

3. _____

4. _____

5. _____

6. _____

7. _____

8. _____

9. _____

10. _____

NOTE: Visit www.KLSWebSolutions.com/Worksheets to print new copies of the worksheets contained in this book.

It was a matter of necessity for retail, travel and cell phone companies. They had no choice but to fully adopt the Internet because of overwhelming consumer demand. If these companies wanted to stay in business, they had to create an Internet presence. Barnes & Noble is still smarting over the hit they took from a little blip on the radar screen called Amazon.com. Are you going to wait until your competition is stealing your clients before you build a site or revamp the current one you have?

CPAs and service professionals have been very slow to adopt the Internet for client development purposes. I can tell you from firsthand experience, they are missing the boat. As a result, those that start now have a reasonable opportunity for growing their practice and profitability.

And what about those who ignore the Internet and its value for developing new clients, selling more services and retaining current clients? They lag behind, wondering what went wrong.

Is it worth it for you? What you need to take into consideration is the value of your clients versus the cost (monetary and intangible) for web site investment, opportunities and timing.

Lifetime Client Value

CPAs love numbers, right? Grab a pen and let's run the figures. Let's do a very rough, quick calculation of the value of a new client. Using the space below, first estimate the annual revenue you make from a new client. Is it $5,000? $15,000? $25,000? Now, estimate the lifespan of a new client. This is the number of years a client will remain (on average) with your firm. By multiplying the average annual revenue by the lifespan of your client, you can calculate a very rough estimate of the lifetime value of your new client.

For example, if you receive an average of $50,000 a year in fees from a new client and your average retention rate is ten years, then $500,000 is a rough estimate of your client value. If your retention rate is 15 years, then the value climbs up to $750,000.

Next, multiply that figure times the number of new clients you expect to gain over the course of a year.

Lifetime Client Value Calculations

Estimated Annual Revenue from New Clients: $_____

x

Estimated Client Lifespan: _____ years

=

Estimate Lifetime Value of One Client: $_____

x

Number of Expected New Clients Annually: _____

=

Total Estimated Annual Revenue From Lifetime Clients:

$_____

Web Site Investment

Now let's compare the value of the clients you would normally receive with the possible costs associated with creating or revamping a web site.

Many times when I meet with a prospective client, they tell me that they don't plan to use their web site for client development. Their reason for web creation or redesign is simply because they want to see a web site for their business online. They feel they need a site, but have no clue what to do with it or what it can do for them.

The CPAs that begin to use their web site for client development and retention will be at a huge advantage over their competition. Later on, we will discuss the business opportunities on the Internet in detail, but let's quickly highlight them here.

Client Development: The first real benefit is gaining potential clients — within your own town and around the globe — who are searching for your services.

If constructed properly, your site can work as a 24/7 lead generation tool. Your web site can:

- bring in traffic
- guide visitors to the pages most appropriate for them
- answer questions
- provide detailed information
- build credibility
- provide company history
- deliver forms
- offer updates and changes in tax laws
- and so much more!

In addition, the Internet can dramatically increase your reach. Lead generation that was once limited to local or regional networking events and the occasional convention or conference is now increased exponentially. Your site knows no geographic boundaries, unless you set them. You can attract visitors from across the country or around the globe if you choose to. Think for a moment what that would do to those estimated figures you jotted down on the previous page. How many more annual new clients would you be able to land?

Even if this were the only benefit of good web design, it would be well worth it. However, there are so many other things a properly designed site can do for your company.

Shorten the Sales Cycle: While those people you meet at networking events **may** be interested in your services, it is practically guaranteed your web site visitors **will** be. Why? Because they searched you out instead of the opposite being true. This immediately shortens your sales cycle so that a prospect becomes a client much faster. Your web site gives your potential clients all the information about your firm so that they feel comfortable with you before ever making contact with you.

With networking, you meet a person (or perhaps receive their business card at a conference or convention). You contact them in an effort to land a phone or in-person meeting. Many times, you are shot down before you ever get that far. If you do arrange a meeting, it still isn't guaranteed you'll get the account. Questions are asked; information is requested; concerns are voiced. All of these things require your personal attention (that takes up hours and hours of your non-billable time). It's a long, costly process. But not if you let your web site lead the way. You save countless hours and countless dollars over the course of a year due to reduced client acquisition expenses alone.

Client Retention & Growth: At the beginning of this chapter, we discussed the lifetime value of a client and its importance for your revenue stream. The more that you can lengthen your retention rate, the better off you are. Why? Because, according to the Microsoft Small Business Center, it costs five times more to gain a new client than it does to retain an existing one.

Think about that. Take the figures in your Estimated Annual Revenue From Lifetime Clients and multiply it by a factor of five. That's how much more your firm could be bringing in if you had a web site to mine your existing client base for additional revenue. How? Several ways actually. Automated emails, updated information and services pages, and any number of other ways that web-based technology can keep your clients abreast of what you currently offer along with any new services you add. You'll be amazed at how many of your existing clients had no clue you offered all the services you do.

The Time Is Now

Those CPAs that begin to view and use their web sites to market their businesses will be at an advantage. At this point in time there is a low level of competition on the Internet among CPA sites. Sure, a large percentage of CPA firms have web sites, but having a web site and making full use of the web in order to benefit your firm are two entirely different things. If you move now, you can take advantage of:

Easier Search Engine Positioning: While search engine optimization (the practice of helping sites show at the top of the search results) encompasses many factors, success is partially due to the level of competing sites. How many other sites are trying to rank in the same positions you are trying to rank for? Right now, not many. Most CPAs have not yet caught on to using this strategy to find new clients. The sooner your web site is created and optimized, the more stable you'll be in the rankings. There is a lot to be said for being a frontrunner in the area of search engine optimization. (More about this in an upcoming chapter.)

Pay-Per-Click: Have you ever noticed the "sponsored ads" at the top of Yahoo! or to the right side of Google? Those are called pay-per-click ads. The name comes from the business model of the search engine. Each time someone types in a keyword ("CPA" for example) or a keyphrase ("corporate CPA services" perhaps) on one of those ads, the advertiser has to pay a fee to the search engine. The fees are based on a bidding schedule of keywords and phrases. Each time a searcher types in one of the keywords an advertiser has listed in his account, the paid ad is displayed. So, obviously, the ads targeting the least competitive keywords will cost less than those that target highly competitive keywords. (**NOTE:** The terms "keywords" and "keyphrases" are commonly interchanged.)

Right now, there is not much competition for most keywords that apply to CPA firms. This won't last long. As more CPAs decide to create or develop their sites to meet full potential, this will begin to change and change quickly. Smart accountants will take advantage of the low cost now and incorporate a pay-per-click strategy into their marketing mix.

Sales Vehicle: Think about this for a moment. What steps are involved in bringing a prospect from the lead generation stage through the sales process and into the standing of being an official client of your firm?

Usually countless hours of networking, schmoozing and meetings would be required just to get the business cards or contact information for individuals or companies who **might** be interested in your firm. With the creation of your new website, the entire process is turned on its head. Potential clients that have a viable and current need are seeking you out and finding you as they search for accounting services online. Simply put: the Internet becomes another sales vehicle.

You are at a big advantage here as well. The current CPA sites online just don't cut it. They have no sales strategy and no well thought out method of enticing clients once they reach the site. You, on the other hand, will be much more organized because you had the good sense to buy this book! This, too, will save you money and increase your bottom line profits because you will have a much more effective site than other CPAs have.

Ezines: For the most part, CPAs hate to write. For this reason, very few CPA web sites offer automated information updates, such as ezines (electronic magazines), to their clients or prospects. Creating and publicizing your ezine (also called a newsletter) is yet another strategy to add to your web site lineup. Low levels of competition in this area mean you'll likely have more than your fair share of subscribers (who can then convert to clients). Ezines will be discussed in detail later on.

In conclusion, remember that the Internet isn't going anywhere. Each and every year we see exponential growth with additional individual and business users either coming online or increasing their Internet use. Yes, you could ignore the Internet and keep doing business the way you always have. But why? The benefits clearly outweigh the costs. You've seen that from your own calculations a few pages back.

As we move forward, we'll get into more detail about each area of your site. You'll discover what is mandatory and what is optional. You'll see recommended strategies for success and be warned of pitfalls guaranteed to drag you under. Use the worksheets. Take your own notes. Jot down any additional questions you have. When we're done, you'll be fully prepared to work with a web designer to achieve the goals you listed.

3

Do You Google?

*"Suppose I could program my computer to create a space
in which anything could be linked to anything.
There would be a single global information space."*
Tim Berners-Lee
Founder of the World Wide Web

As we discussed in the previous chapter, the Internet is having a huge effect on us all. If you think about it, one of the biggest factors has been because of search engines.

In all actuality, the Internet was invented (in its first and very crude form) in 1962 with the aid of several scientists and the US Air Force. By the 1970s, a couple of brave computer nerds actually began using this new technology when they published information on the ARPANET (as it was then called). From there the Internet grew at lightning speed over the next 19 years in the business, scientific and military sectors. The Internet didn't receive its high acclaim until the doors burst wide open with the invention of Yahoo! — the first search engine. Yahoo! made it possible to easily "surf the Internet" and make functional use of all the information stored in its databases. Suddenly, finding a web site was no big deal.

From those humble beginnings, we now find that 60 million US Internet users make some use of a search engine every day, an increase of 55% from 2004 according to a study conducted by Pew Internet & American Life Project in November 2005. Amazing!

People now use the Internet to search for products and information, and — believe it or not — even professional services for themselves or their businesses. Your web site can be used to find people that are **searching** for you or your services.

Search Engines

Just to make sure that we are all on the same page, let's define the term "search engine." Here is what I found in www.wikipedia.com:

A search engine is a program designed to help find information stored on a computer system such as the World Wide Web, or a personal computer. The search engine allows one to ask for content meeting specific criteria (typically those containing a given word or phrase) and retrieves a list of references that match those criteria. Search engines use regularly updated indexes to operate quickly and efficiently. Without further qualification, search engine usually refers to a Web search engine, which searches for information on the public Web.

When people conduct Internet searches, they rarely go beyond the first two or three pages. If you want to be noticed in the results of the search engines, you need to appear in the top 10-15 listings. This may seem like an impossible task, considering how many web sites are out there, but it can be achieved if you do it right. We will be covering this in detail later in this book.

Search Demographics

A couple of years ago, Google posted demographics of its users on its site. Here are some select findings from the information they provided:

- 59% have at least completed college.
- Average income is above $77,000 annually.
- 73% have online experience of 4+ years.
- 54% are online every day.

What does this tell us about people who use Google? They are mostly well educated and upper, middle class. A lot of them go on the Internet every day, and they are very familiar with using search engines. Many of these individuals are business owners or are the decision makers at businesses. Are these the types of people that you might like to sell your services to? You can reach them effectively when your site is positioned well in the Google search engine.

How to Use Search for Your Firm

As we mentioned in a previous chapter, people are questioning authority more and more. If a doctor tells someone that s/he has an illness, many head immediately to the search engines to find out more about the illness and the various treatments. Many businesses and individuals are doing the same thing with the professional advice that they get from their CPAs.

A great way to capitalize on this activity is to include articles, white papers or entire web pages dedicated to topics in which people are most interested. This not only helps your current client base by keeping them updated, but it is also a wonderful lead generation tool.

For example, let's say a person is searching the Internet for information about tax-deductible travel expenses. They come across an article on your web site that addresses this subject. The surfer begins to read the article and is highly impressed with your firm's apparent knowledge and sense of authority on the topic. She reads intently and begins to think about how she would really like a firm on this level to handle her business needs. Next thing you know, you have a new prospect!

What a great way to be introduced. You are not approaching them at a networking event to try and get their business. They are approaching you because you are providing information they need while — at the same time — positioning yourself as an expert. Win-win!

Here's a case in point.

Case Study — Elizabeth Brown, CPA

Elizabeth Brown is a sole practitioner CPA in Westchester County, New York. Elizabeth serves a select client base of small- to medium-sized businesses, helping them improve their companies through a variety of financial services, achieve greater tax savings and better financial controls, and maintain federal and state compliance.

When Elizabeth first approached me about redesigning her web site, she explained that she really wasn't planning to use the site for client development. All the same, she felt she should have a web site to promote her business because other CPAs she knew of had web sites. Elizabeth's site at the time we met didn't have a professional look. In fact, it actually detracted from the appearance she was trying to portray. While Elizabeth wasn't directing any potential clients to the site (or building any search engine rankings), she did want the site to be of value to those who used it.

My firm created a very basic site for Elizabeth to represent her practice. It had all the elements of good web design (that we will talk about in subsequent chapters) plus the coding was search engine friendly giving her greater potential for high rankings.

Within six months, Elizabeth was contacted by several prospective clients in the Westchester County area that found her web site on the Internet. Her reaction?

> "Most of my clients have come from referrals. Now I have new clients finding me through the search engines as well. I would have never guessed I could acquire as many good, new clients through the Internet."
>
> *– Elizabeth Brown*

Search engines are a vital part of business and personal life. That means they play an important role in the lives of your prospective clients, too. When you create or improve your web site, don't neglect the search engines.

Make a note now to discuss search engine optimization with your designer. Many web design firms offer search engine optimization (SEO) friendly designs. Others actually do full optimization. In later chapters, I'll explain the ins and outs of SEO, but for now, realize its importance to your site and plan to include SEO in your overall strategy.

4
Finding the "Right" Clients

"Success is neither magical nor mysterious. Success is the natural consequence of consistently applying the basic fundamentals."

Jim Rohn
US Business Executive

Search engines can send a lot of new leads to your web site. However, as you very well know, not all leads are created equal. Some leads may never turn into clients, and some prospects may not even be the type of client you are looking for. When planning your web site, you want to ensure (as much as possible) that those who contact you are a good fit with your firm. This helps you eliminate wasted time with those who might not be the right clients for you.

How do you do this? First, define the criteria for your clients, and then design your web site to meet their needs while weeding out visitors that do not fit your criteria.

Perfect Clients

If you could describe your "perfect" client, what would you say? Most likely you would include the following two attributes for sure.

Gladly Pay Your Invoices: This seems so obvious, yet many forget the importance of this fundamental concept. I believe there are two sets of clients: those that are happy to pay the invoices and those that can pay the invoices.

We all have those clients who are more than able to pay our invoices, but are constantly complaining about the fee. They are focused on how much they must pay you. These are the clients that you probably don't serve as well as you could because you are always trying to do their work in a hurry. If you don't rush to finish in what they feel is an appropriate amount of time, you end up eating part of your fees or arguing with them over how much time a project took. Perfect clients are happy to pay your invoices. They appreciate the value of your services and understand that consulting, planning, tax preparation and meetings are all tasks that should be compensated for.

In *101 Marketing Strategies for Accounting, Law, Consulting and Professional Service Firms*, Troy Waugh notes that Texans call people who live the life of the rich and famous (but who have no real wealth) "big hat, no cattle." Waugh urges firms to take notice of the clients that they have. Do those clients have the resources to pay your fees and grow with you or are they "big hat, no cattle"? Perfect clients can easily afford your bill.

Ready to Hire You: A perfect client needs your services in the very near future. Someone who is looking for tax services in May (and who just filed their return in April) is probably not going to move very quickly in changing tax advisors.

Your perfect clients will have ongoing personal or business needs. They'll understand the advantage of staying in touch and conducting annual (or quarterly) evaluations to stay abreast of their current financial standing. They will also know that — even if a current and pressing need does not exist — they need to move forward to give your firm time to review their financial records so you will be ready when a need does arise.

Who Is Your Target Market?: Another name for "perfect clients" or "right clients" is "target market." Before you can know when you find a perfect client, you have to have a good idea of who they are and how they behave. It's hard to identify something or someone you know nothing about.

You may think this seems counterintuitive. Why would you want to limit your business to a thin slice of businesses or individuals? Don't you want to sell your CPA services to everyone? The short and blatant answer is no!

In the book *Purple Cow*, Seth Godin tells the story of a friend, Tracey, who was a publicist that started her own business. She sent out hundreds of form letters to marketing directors in an effort to drum up business. She got little response. Since her background was in pharmaceuticals, Godin suggested she focus not just in the area of marketing directors, but specifically on plastic surgeons. Tracey decided to focus and take Godin's advice because she knew all the journals, all the conferences and most of the doctors due to her pharmaceutical background. She is now considered the one and only choice for handling publicity matters for plastic surgeons. She found her target audience — her perfect clients — and made a vital connection with them. It all worked out to her benefit. You can do the same.

How do you set about defining your target audience? It takes a good bit of time, a little research and a lot of observation.

Using the worksheet on the following page, begin to outline who your perfect clients are. This information will be vitally important to your web designer and your copywriter. They will have to know whom you are trying to reach before they can create effective designs and text for your site.

It may be a good idea to make copies of the worksheet before you begin. Be prepared to spend some time on this exercise. It is similar to reviewing a new client's past financial records. Without knowing who they are, what they do, how much they make and what current standing they are in, you can hardly advise them effectively or prepare tax documents on their behalf. Likewise, until you know whom you want to reach via your site, you can't create a site to reach them.

What if you don't have the answers to the questions? Ask! Conduct an informal survey of your current perfect clients to get the information. They'll be flattered that you think so highly of them!

Target Audience Analysis Worksheet

Think about those clients you currently have that you consider to be outstanding clients. These are clients you would love to have a practice full of. If you currently don't have any clients you consider to be perfect, think about what traits they might have. With these people in mind, answer the following questions.

What do these clients have in common? (corporation vs. small business, industry, personality, income, etc.)

_____

_____

_____

Describe as many traits about them (as a group) as you can. (male/female, job title, hobbies, investment types, lifestyle, etc.)

_____

_____

_____

If you didn't list job titles, do it now. What are the job titles of your perfect clients?

_____

_____

_____

What problems do these people face that your firm can solve? (Think about the client here. You want to list the problems **they** face. Do not make a list of your services.)

_____

_____

_____

Why would these clients come to your firm as opposed to another that offers the same or similar services?

_____

_____

_____

What end results will these clients receive after working with your firm? (How will you solve their problems you listed on the previous page?)

_____

_____

_____

Where are these clients in the buying process? (Are they trying to decide if they want to switch providers? Have they decided and are now comparing options?)

_____

_____

_____

Your web designer and copywriter will both benefit greatly from as much information as you can provide for them. The more they know about them, the better they will be able to construct a site that draws the prospective client in and holds their interest.

To that end, let's delve deeper into your target client's personality and behavior. With regard to job titles and other client information above, look at the brief descriptions of the DISC Behavioral Model profiles on the next page and determine which **two profiles** most aptly fit your perfect clients.

1) _____

2) _____

If you need additional space, make copies of this worksheet or use notebook paper.

NOTE: Visit www.KLSWebSolutions.com/Worksheets to print worksheets from the Internet.

Dominance

The Dominance behavioral style is usually described with the following attributes:

- high ego
- problem solver
- likes challenges
- drives hard for results
- positive
- loves power and authority
- motivated by direct answers

You will normally find Dominance types working in fields such as corporate officers, managers, the military, some salespeople, many entrepreneurs, and almost any other person who is in a position or mindset of "control."

Those high in Dominance have a big picture mentality. They are power players who cut to the chase and don't mince words. Dominance types don't have time for small talk, and they don't mix business with pleasure. You won't find these players asking about the kids or inviting you over to the house for drinks. They are all business.

Dominance types want the bottom line first and details afterwards IF they feel details are warranted. Most often they are the visionaries who come up with the plans. They always let others worry about the details of how to make it happen; therefore, details are not always warranted or needed when dealing with a Dominance client.

Show them how you can solve problems. Tell them how you're able to help them reach their goals. Let them know you can handle all the detail work that frees them up to move forward and close in on yet another conquest.

Influence

The Influence behavioral style can be described like this:

- socially and verbally aggressive
- always talking, big on chitchat
- optimistic
- can see the big picture
- people-oriented
- fast mover
- motivated by praise and strokes

Usually Influence types work as salespeople, realtors, hair stylists or other professions where they interact with people constantly.

Influence types can see the big picture, but they aren't the ones that create the big picture. Similarly to Dominance types, those high in Influence are fast movers. But that's where the similarities end.

High "I" types are extremely social. They are verbally aggressive (read: will talk your ears off!) and are big on chitchat. The eternal optimist, Influence types are very people-oriented and are motivated by praise and strokes to their egos. Give them pats on the back for making the right choice in their decision about a CPA and you'll have a friend for life.

Steadiness

Those who fall into the Steadiness behavioral style usually are described as:

- loyal to those they identify with
- good listeners
- patient
- love security
- want to see benefits
- oriented towards family activities
- motivated towards traditional procedures

Steadiness types can typically be found in jobs including small business owners, managers, teachers, bookkeepers and so on.

These are your typical consumer shoppers. Those high in Steadiness make up 40% of the population and are — by far — the largest group of the four types. You'll need to show them the benefits of working with your firm. They'll want to know about your longevity and success rate. They see time for socialization, but are also concentrated on not making a wrong decision. Reassurance is key.

Compliance

The last of the four styles is Compliance. These people usually have the following attributes:

- critical thinkers
- high standards
- well disciplined
- accurate
- motivated by the right way to proceed

You'll find a lot of Compliance types working as CPAs, attorneys, scientists, doctors and the like. Those high in Compliance are geared toward quality. They don't care to purchase the latest and greatest things. Instead, they'd rather wait until a product, service or company proves itself worthy of their patronage.

Quality is high on their list of likes, and they are motivated by proceeding in a logical, orderly fashion toward a predefined, measurable goal. Show them you can take them there and you've got them hooked.

Keep in mind that any group behavioral profiling technique is based on stereotypes. Also note that people are made up of some attributes from all four types. Choosing the two that most likely represent your perfect clients gives you a broader range to work with in your target audience analysis.

Once you have a good idea of who your perfect client is, you can use your web site to qualify those who visit your site. You need to ensure that your web site weeds through the many visitors and sends you only the best.

Qualify With Your Web Site

OK, so we have defined what we want the web site to qualify: the right type of client, those ready to use your services, and those willing and able to pay your invoices. How do we get your web site to do this for you so that you are only going to hear from highly qualified leads? There are three main areas in your web site that can be used to accomplish this:

1. Copy on the Home Page

2. Information provided on the Our Clients Page

3. Questions on the Contact Us Form

4. A descriptive Services Page

While you will most certainly have other pages on your site, these three will offer the most help in guiding the right prospects to contact you.

Home Page

The home page is normally the first page your visitors will see. While web surfers can reach other pages of your site before the home page, generally this is the most often looked at page. Many visitors never make it past the home page for a variety of reasons, so it is important to make the best use of this space on your site in order to guide visitors in the ways you want them to go. With this in mind, you need to ensure you define what type of client you are looking for right on your home page.

For example, if your target market is high net worth individuals, then your web site's home page should clearly state that these are the people you serve. The design elements, the copy (text), the graphics or photos . . . everything on the home page should cater to high net worth individuals.

If your perfect clients are accounting managers at large corporations, this needs to be indicated on the home page using the same elements: copy, design and graphics/images. You want your target audience to feel right at home when they reach your site. If you had guests visiting in your home, you would take time to make a special effort to ensure their stay would be welcoming. You might buy snacks or drinks you know they enjoyed. You would plan activities they would appreciate. You would have meals consisting of their favorite foods. The same applies to the visitors to your site. Always remember:

It's Not About You; It's All About Them!

Contrary to popular belief, your site should not be designed to meet your preferences. Everything to do with your site from color selection to how long the copy is should be in answer to the question, "What would our target audience prefer?" This starts with the home page.

Our Clients Page

There is no big secret when it comes to your client list. If your competitors are worth their salt, they already know who your clients are. Just like you know who theirs are. Don't be afraid to list your clients and their industry specialties on your web site. By giving visitors to your site a listing of your clients, you will help in further qualifying them. Visitors will take a look at the list of your clients and either resonate with it or not. Again, your site is doing the work for you by pre-qualifying prospective clients who contact you.

Of course, you need to check with your clients and make sure they authorize you to use their names on your web site. You can make this an advantage for them by providing a link from your site to their web site (if they have one). This will aid in driving traffic to their site and will aid in helping them achieve higher positioning in the search engines.

One of my CPA clients included a testimonial on her site from a large company she provided services for. She included the name of the company owner along with the business name. She received an instant new client when a visitor to her site read the testimonial. He knew the business owner who provided the comments and — because he trusted the business owner's opinion — he contacted the CPA and hired her on the spot.

If you really prefer not to list your clients — or you're just starting out and don't have many clients — then list your industry specialties and the types of clients you work with. This will give your visitors a general idea of your preferred business types.

Contact Us Page

If a visitor to your site has made it to this page, they are interested in your firm. This is a big step. Business professionals are pretty savvy on the Internet. Many have given up their email addresses only to be bombarded with unauthorized email ("spam" as it is affectionately called). If they fill out the form on your Contact Us page, it means your site has instilled trust; your message resonates with them, and they are willing to take the next step.

On a basic level, your Contact Us form should have a minimal amount of information to be filled out. The more simple-looking the form the more likely your prospect is going to take the time to complete it. Put yourself in the visitor's shoes. How much information are **you** willing to divulge on a site? To start with, keep the questions down to the absolute minimum. All you really need to know is:

- name
- phone number
- email address

These should be required fields (that is, fields that must be completed in order for the form to work). A couple of other items that are good to know include:

- how did you find us?
- comment or question
- reason for contact

The question about how the visitor found you could include a drop-down menu with options such as "Search Engine: Google," "Search Engine: Yahoo!," "Referral from_____," etc. The comment/question box should be left open-ended, so the visitor can type whatever s/he needs to. The "reason for contact" section can include a drop-down menu of your services they can choose from. None of these three should be required fields. They should all be noted as optional.

Services Page

In addition, your Services page can help qualify visitors. By simply listing the services you provide with brief descriptions, your visitors will know if you offer what they are looking for. If you don't, they will know to search for someone else who does offer that particular service.

Here is the place to detail what specialties you have, if you work exclusively with a particular industry, if you don't work with a particular industry, etc. Be specific.

I stress that you should give descriptions of each service. Keep in mind: you are the CPA, not your client. They may not know the proper name of a particular service. By offering descriptions, you guide visitors to a better understanding of what is available from your firm. If it is too cumbersome to list everything you offer, then provide the most often used services and make a note on the page that visitors should call to request information about services they don't see listed on your site.

The most important feat is to use these four pages to draw in those considered perfect clients and to hold back others you know you'd rather not work with.

5

Client Development Made Easy

"Marketing and innovation are the two chief functions of business.
You get paid for creating a client, which is marketing.
And you get paid for creating a new dimension of performance,
which is innovation. Everything else is a cost center."

Peter Drucker
U.S. Management Consultant

You're a CPA, so I know that you will easily understand the following concept. Let's say it usually takes you six months to land a $25,000/year client. If you shorten the time it takes to convert the prospect into a client from six months to three months, then you have potentially doubled your revenue for the year.

Shortening your sales cycle is very easy to accomplish through your web site. In fact, client development, selling and client maintenance are three outstanding uses for your site. The web naturally suits these purposes, and, through some solid planning, your site can be built to naturally perform in these areas, too. Let's start at the beginning of the sales cycle and go from client development and prospecting to client maintenance. Once these processes are in place, your site will save you enormous amounts of time with tasks that usually would tie up your schedule.

Client Development & Prospecting

If you currently don't have a web site, or you currently don't use your web site to convert prospects to clients, let's talk about how to change that. How does the process normally play out?

You meet someone at a networking event or you receive a referral from a current client. You may spend some time talking with them over the phone about your services and questions they have. This probably takes you one-half hour to one hour of your time (at least). Now, if they are really interested in your services and they could potentially be a big client, then you are going to spend a lot more time with them to earn their trust. That means you will probably have a meeting with them in their office. You'll ask more questions about their business and tell them more about how your services are just right for them. (OK, how much time did that take? Probably four hours between preparing for the meeting, commuting and the meeting itself.) If the prospect is a larger client, there is probably a request for proposal involved (more non-billable time, more work). You can spend a lot of time with prospective clients to turn them into real clients. None of which generates a return for the effort.

Why do prospects demand so much of your time before they become clients? You know the answer to this — they need to trust you. Hiring a CPA is definitely a big deal. Put yourself in the prospect's shoes. The CPA firm will have access to your most sensitive information. The firm will be responsible for giving you advice on areas in which you may be very vulnerable. The CPA firm will be in charge of your financial future. They will make sure you are in official compliance, so you aren't hit with penalties, fees or — God forbid — an audit! Whether doing individual tax returns, business returns or retirement planning, your financial life is in their hands. This is heavy stuff, and your prospects take it very seriously. They need to make sure they can trust you 100%. It's your job — via your site — to relay that trust, that sense of responsibility and that comfort.

On the worksheet on the following page, list the process you typically go through when courting a new prospect. This information will be helpful to your web designer and copywriter when creating your site because they can incorporate the necessary site structure and navigation in the design plus answer many questions prospects have in the copy. In fact, you'll also find a space for frequently asked questions. Jot down the ones you are most often asked by prospective clients along with the answers to those questions.

Prospecting Process Worksheet

What steps do you normally go through when courting a new prospect? Be as detailed as possible listing the steps from first introduction to official welcome as a new client. (Steps may include: referral from a current client, phone call to referral, meeting with referral, follow-up phone calls, etc.)

1)_____

_____

_____

_____

2)_____

_____

_____

_____

3)_____

_____

_____

_____

4)_____

_____

_____

_____

5)_____

_____

_____

_____

6)_____

_____

_____

_____

7)_____

_____

_____

_____

8)_____

_____

_____

_____

9)_____

_____

_____

_____

10)_____

_____

_____

_____

If you have more than ten steps, make copies of this worksheet or use additional sheets of notebook paper.

NOTE: Visit www.KLSWebSolutions.com/Worksheets to print worksheets from the Internet.

Frequently Asked Questions by Prospects

Below, write the questions you are most often asked by prospective clients along with their answers.

Question: _____

_____

_____

Answer: _____

_____

_____

_____

Question: _____

_____

_____

Answer: _____

_____

_____

_____

Question: _____

_____

_____

Answer: _____

_____

_____

_____

Question: _____

_____

_____

Answer: _____

_____

_____

_____

Question: _____

_____

_____

Answer: _____

_____

_____

_____

If you have more questions, make copies of this worksheet or use additional sheets of notebook paper.

NOTE: Visit www.KLSWebSolutions.com/Worksheets to print worksheets from the Internet.

Building Credibility

How, exactly, does a site project credibility and build trust? Several ways, actually, including its design, copy and functionality.

How many times have you been to a site that looked as though some 12-year-old designed it? The images were blurry and warped. The colors were atrocious. The copy was loud and used way too many exclamation points. There were misspellings, links that did not work (called broken links) and forms that were complicated to complete, if they worked at all. All these things added up to a feeling that this company was not very trustworthy. Take a look around the Internet. The next time you find yourself surfing, take some notes about which sites you felt were credible and which were not. Why did you think that way? You probably had no exposure to the site until recently. Yet, something gave you a sense that a particular site worked. What was it? Those are the elements you want to include in your own site.

There are many ways to build credibility. A few include:

- professional-looking design
- well-written copy that speaks in the language of your target audience
- links that work consistently
- forms that are easy to use and function as they should
- testimonials from well-known and respected sources
- information (articles, white papers, briefs) that are authoritative and accurate
- ezines (newsletters) that appeal to prospects

Others certainly exist, including listings of clients and/or references and case studies about how your firm has helped various clients achieve their goals. Include several of these (if not all of them) to help your site appear more credible in the eyes of your visitors.

Use the worksheet on the next page to list sites you have visited and liked. List why these sites made you feel a sense of trust and/or why you felt the site was credible. Which of the elements above did they include?

Credible Sites Worksheet

Note: A URL (also called a domain name) starts with "www." and can end with ".com," ".net," ".org," ".info" or others.

Site 1

URL: www._____ . _____

This site gave me a sense of credibility and trust because

_____
_____
_____

It used the following elements:

professional design	well-written copy	active links
easy-to-use forms	testimonials	references
case studies	information	ezines

other: _____

Site 2
URL: www._____ . _____

This site gave me a sense of credibility and trust because

_____

_____

_____

It used the following elements:

professional design	well-written copy	active links
easy-to-use forms	testimonials	references
case studies	information	ezines

other: _____

Site 3
URL: www._____ . _____

This site gave me a sense of credibility and trust because

_____

_____

_____

It used the following elements:

professional design   well-written copy   active links

easy-to-use forms   testimonials   references

case studies   information   ezines

other: _____

Site 4
URL: www._____ . _____

This site gave me a sense of credibility and trust because

_____

_____

_____

It used the following elements:

professional design   well-written copy   active links

easy-to-use forms   testimonials   references

case studies   information   ezines

other: _____

Site 5
URL: www._____ . _____

This site gave me a sense of credibility and trust because

_____

_____

_____

It used the following elements:

professional design	well-written copy	active links
easy-to-use forms	testimonials	references
case studies	information	ezines

other: _____

If you need additional space, make copies of this worksheet or use notebook paper.

NOTE: Visit www.KLSWebSolutions.com/Worksheets to print worksheets from the Internet.

Selling

As much as you don't want to think about it, you have to sell your services to every new client you get. Most CPAs find the idea of selling distasteful. They would rather be able to live off referrals. However, do you realize that when you get a referral, you've actually sold something? That's right! You had to sell your current client on your services, your abilities, your competence and more before s/he would make the referral. Referrals are a vital source of revenue for CPAs.

A large percentage of CPAs that I interviewed for this book felt that at least 90% of their new business was from word of mouth from existing clients. Current clients are a major pipeline for new business. This increases their value exponentially and puts an even higher value on client loyalty. But, let's not digress.

Selling doesn't have to be distasteful. In fact, selling, if done properly, doesn't even seem like selling at all. I call it, the "very subtle sell." It can be difficult to pull off, but with trained professionals at your side, your site can attract new clients without them (or you!) feeling like they've been "sold." Plus your site will help you re-sell your current clients, as you add new services and will help you get more referrals from more sources.

So what is the "very subtle sell"? It is your web site giving a prospective client everything that they need on both a conscious and unconscious level, so they naturally feel an attraction to your firm.

Once you have gained their trust with your web site, then you need to provide them the information they are looking for. Notice that I am not saying you just provide them with arbitrary information. I'm saying you provide the **specific information they are looking for**. There is a big difference. A web site that provides visitors with specific information they need will shorten your sales cycle and convert prospects into clients. What information is that? The answer can be found in the target audience analysis you've completed along with worksheets you've filled out. Do you see how one thing builds on another? By the time we're finished, you'll have a complete outline of your site to hand to your designer and copywriter. With the information you provide, they should be able to create a site to meet or exceed your goals. So, let's keep moving forward.

Client Maintenance

I brushed the topic of client loyalty earlier. I don't want to neglect that subject because it is so important to all steps of the selling process.

Clients need to be treated like gold. Not only do they provide you with income, but they also provide you with the opportunity for more business through up-selling additional services and new clients through referrals. In earlier chapters, we discussed how clients are becoming less and less trusting of the professionals in their lives, but the good news is that you can use your web site and the Internet to counter that lack of trust. Your web site can actually help cement your relationship with your clients.

Experts estimate it costs at least four to five times as much to get a new client as it does to keep an existing client. Also, in a recent study of client buying behavior, analysts at RainToday.com found that more than half of professional service purchasers are open to switching service providers. That is a scary statistic. Client loyalty cannot be taken for granted at all in this day and age. The more communication you have with your clients, the more trust is established. The more trust that is established, the more the client will think of you as a business partner rather than a vendor.

How can your site help with accomplishing this? Through the use of web-based tools designed to encourage client loyalty automatically. One is a Client Only section. Another primary way is through the use of ezines (electronic magazines).

Client Only Section

A client only section can very easily be set up so that only your clients can enter this area of the site. The client would be given a login name and a password. When clients enter this section of the site, they would be able to download forms and materials that you usually mail to them. They could find updated reports, instructions, articles specific to their industry or whatever you choose to include.

For example, an email can be automatically generated and sent to clients reminding them to login to your web site to download a particular form that they need to fill out and send back to you. You would only need to send one email rather than dozens, hundreds or thousands of letters via postal mail.

The client only section of your site can be a tremendous time-saver for you and your clients. And, it certainly would help with client maintenance and client loyalty.

Blogs

Blogs are web sites or web pages with highly editorial content. The sheer opinion of the site owner is published on the blog on a daily basis. Site visitors are then welcomed to make comments or give alternative opinions. Blogs can be good marketing tools in certain circumstances, if you are able to maintain the blog and update it daily. If you don't have the time or content to contribute to a blog, I would not recommend adding one to your marketing plan.

Ezines (Electronic Magazines)

First developed around 1994, ezines (pronounced E'-zeens) are electronic versions of magazines. They get their name because they generally have different sections including: Welcome or Letter from the Editor, articles, resources, updates and more. Also referred to as online newsletters, ezines come in all shapes and sizes. They can be formatted in plain text or HTML (with pictures and colors). Ezines are delivered to email boxes rather than traditional mailboxes. In

January 2006

Kaja's Design Tips
The Home Designer's Resource

Dear Kaja,
Welcome to the **Kaja Gam Design E-Zine.** Here you'll find tips and ideas to help you tackle your home improvement projects.

The Kitchen of Today

by Kaja Gam   Is this the year to remodel your kitchen? According to House & Garden magazine's January 2006 special report, the kitchen has doubled in size since the 1970s. That means it finally gets the recognition it deserves as the most important room in the house. Kitchens designed today will last for a very long time because of their new innovations including efficient space layout, hi-tech appliances, cabinet components and durable materials. All this makes for a functional, convenient and beautiful living space. From floor to ceiling, here's what you need to know about the kitchen of your dreams.

The kitchen is integral to our lives. Everyone in the home makes use of this room. The name "kitchen" and the image of the housewife donning an apron and toiling away behind closed doors are history. Many attempts at naming this new multi-functional room have been made: great room, family all-room and eat-live kitchen just begin to describe the function of this central hub of our lives.

What they all sum up is the same reality: the kitchen is the axis of our lives. Entertaining friends, spending time with family, talking about the day's events and cooking up a little romance are all done in the kitchen. Read More...

View kitchens designed by Kaja.

Next Month's Topic

Create Your Own Mudroom
If your house doesn't have a mudroom, it should. And it can! Find out how to transform current space into this necessary space.

fact, you probably are subscribed to a few ezines yourself. If not, take a look at the samples below to get an idea of what ezines are.

You'll notice they all have common characteristics whether they are HTML (with graphics) or plain old text.

PostCards from the web

Hi Everyone-PostCards from the web is a monthly newsnote geared towards small businesses but I hope that everyone can find some useful information.

This issue focuses on tools for spotting the latest trends from consumer demand to interest rates to movies!

Travel Tips: Have you set your business goals for 2006? Even if you have, you may want to check out **Trendwatching**. This site enlists over 7,000 "trend spotters" all over the world. These spotters look for emerging consumer trends and related business ideas. **Sign-up for the no-cost email that includes real-world business examples and great advice on the latest trends.**

Best Bets: The **Blog Pulse Trend Tool** is another spot to check for emerging trends. You enter three words or phrases and the tool will graphically display how frequently those words have appeared in the blogs over the past two, four or six months. **Read more about the tool...**

Favorite Spots: The **Iowa Electronic Market**, the first prediction market, was created in 1988 by the University of Iowa. It was correct every time. **They also have a newer market that predicts how Federal Reserve Policy will affect interest rates. Always good to know!**

Fun Spots: Predict what movies will be successful at the **Hollywood Stock Exchange**. Visitors buy and sell virtual shares of celebrities and movies with Hollywood Dollars. This takes the cake!

Have a great 2006!

Visit us at www.mustangwebdesigns.com

January 2006
Kaja's Design Tips
The Home Designer's Resource

Dear Kaja,

Welcome to the Kaja
Gam Design E-Zine. Here you'll find tips and
ideas to help you tackle
your home improvement projects.

~~~~~~

The Kitchen of Today
by Kaja Gam

Is this the year to remodel your kitchen? According
to House & Garden magazine's January 2006 special
report, the kitchen has doubled in size since the
1970s. That means it finally gets the recognition it
deserves as the most important room in the house.
Kitchens designed today will last for a very long time
because of their new innovations including efficient
space layout, hi-tech appliances, cabinet
components and durable materials. All this makes for
a functional, convenient and beautiful living space.
From floor to ceiling, here's what you need to know
about the kitchen of your dreams.

The kitchen is integral to our lives. Everyone in the
home makes use of this room. The name "kitchen"
and the image of the housewife donning an apron
and toiling away behind closed doors are history.
Many attempts at naming this new multi-functional
room have been made: great room, family all-room
and eat-live kitchen just begin to describe the
function of this central hub of our lives.

What they all sum up is the same reality: the
kitchen is the axis of our lives. Entertaining friends,
spending time with family, talking about the day's
events and cooking up a little romance are all done in
the kitchen.

Ezines are fabulous for maintaining client loyalty, promoting additional services, generating client referrals, introducing new services or employees and keeping in touch. Don't think those are important? Think again!

A Weber State University study of why clients switch CPAs showed the number one reason given was that the CPA was not proactive in delivering services.

As stated earlier, it costs four to five times less to sell to existing clients than to bring in new clients. According to an article by Allan Boress, published by the AICPA, "Unlike the 90 percent of their peers, the top business producers in the accounting profession generate approximately 25 percent to 40 percent of their new, incremental business from the sales of additional services to their existing clients." Most CPAs are absolutely shocked at the fact that their client base has no idea about all the services they provide. The CPAs had no clue that a portion of their business was walking right out the door because existing clients simply didn't know those services were offered. That loss is easily preventable with your ezine.

Keep in Touch

Depending on the clients, they may not have a need to be in constant contact with you. However, you almost certainly have a need to be in constant contact with them. Keeping your name in front of clients helps cement the relationship. It reminds them of whom to call for their accounting needs. It gives them a feeling that you're concerned about them and want to keep them up to date on important changes that might affect their well-being.

A Small Business Administration survey reports that 68% of clients who stop doing business with a company make that decision because they feel unappreciated. Don't let your clients feel unappreciated. There's no reason for that. Especially when you can develop an automated ezine to encourage loyalty, express your appreciation and keep in touch.

Business Referrals

Ezines are an excellent tool for generating referrals. Including a simple reminder for subscribers to forward your ezine to their associates and friends who might find it useful can lead to referrals. Publicly thanking clients in your ezine for their referrals can trigger others to think of people or companies they can also refer to you.

Ezines are also economical: no stamps, no stationery and no envelopes. Is there a cheaper way to keep in touch with all of your clients? Plus, as I mentioned, they are automated so — once you generate a template — you can quickly create ezines every month with little trouble.

We'll discuss the actual creation of ezines in a later chapter, but for now, realize that these can be very productive tools for client development, sales and client maintenance.

6

80% Planning, 20% Doing

*"Spectacular achievement is always
preceded by painstaking preparation."*
Roger Staubach
Dallas Cowboys Quarterback
& Real Estate Entrepreneur

Your firm spends a lot of time on planning. You plan for audits; you encourage clients to do tax planning, and you encourage business owners to plan for their retirements. You know the importance of planning. You need to place the same emphasis on planning your web site.

The 80/20 Rule

In Richard Koch's book, *The 80/20 Principle*, this principle is defined as a minority of causes, inputs or efforts that usually lead to a majority of the results, outputs or rewards. Koch further states that, in business, many examples of the 80/20 Principle have been validated. Twenty percent of products usually account for about 80 percent of dollar sales value. Twenty percent of your clients account for 80% of the revenues. I've seen this in action: many accountants that I interviewed for this book believe that roughly 20% of their clients accounted for 80% of their gross revenue.

Using the 80/20 rule, I would assert that you need to spend 80

49

percent of your time planning your web site project. The remaining 20% of the time will be spent actually doing the design, writing, development, etc. It will all come together SO much easier when the necessary time is spent on the front end of the project.

Experts say that every minute spent planning saves a firm between two to forty minutes in implementation. A well thought out web site will bring you the results you want, save implementation time and, most importantly, save money at every turn.

Begin With the End in Mind

To create an effective web site, you must decide: what results does your firm want from the site? Look back over the worksheet you've completed as well as the target audience analysis. Review the goals you originally listed for your site. When you think about what you want to happen **after** a prospect or customer visits your site, what is foremost on your mind? If you're like most, your answers include:

- Generate Leads: Find prospective clients from the search engines who are searching for your services.
- Shorten Sales Cycle: Aid in the sales cycle by answering questions and building trust.
- Keep in Touch with Clients: Maintain client trust, sell more services and generate referrals.
- Increase Efficiency: Send people to your web site to download forms, get directions to your office, etc.
- Keep in Touch with Prospects: Using your web site or ezine to remind prospects about your firm is an unobtrusive way to keep in touch.

This — all by itself — is quite a list. Before going much further, you'll want to prioritize your goals. You want your message to stay clear and concise throughout the process and that takes planning (of course).

A wonderful example of a company that has remained true to their number one priority is Google. Google's first "business" was providing search capabilities for people looking for information on the web, and if you look at Google's web site, this is clear:

Although Google has expanded its business into a lot of different areas over the years, it is still making sure that searching is the number one priority on its web site. In an interview with *Fast Company* in November 2005, Marissa Mayer, Google's Director of Consumer Web Products, commented on the tension between complexity of function and simplicity of design. "Google has the functionality of a really complicated Swiss Army knife, but the home page is our way of approaching it closed. It's simple; it's elegant; you can slip it in your pocket, but it's got the great doodad when you need it. A lot of our competitors are like a Swiss Army knife open—and that can be intimidating and occasionally harmful."

I believe that this has been the secret to Google's continued success. Unlike the other search engines that are cluttered with so much information that you don't see any of it, Google is easy to use. Be a Google!

Who's in Charge?

Ever go to meetings, where everyone is sitting around brainstorming? The ideas are flowing and everyone feels good. But then, the meeting ends and all the ideas fall to the floor with a loud thud. There is no one to pick up the ball and move it forward. No one was in charge. The same applies to your web site project. Someone needs to be in charge of the site planning and implementation.

If you are a sole entity, I guess you know who is in charge. However, don't try to take on the entire project yourself. You are best served to outsource as much of the tasks as possible. I know small business owners try to save every cent they can, but — because you're not a web designer — I can assure you this is not your area of expertise. Let those with professional experience in this area do their jobs.

If you are in a larger firm, you need to designate one person that has the time or will make the time to oversee your web site project. A team can work together if need be, but one person should have power of final say. If everyone is in charge, the project will quickly become confused. One individual within your firm should be the sole contact for web designers, copywriters, graphic artists, programmers and whoever else will be working to develop your site.

Even with larger firms, I would encourage you to outsource as much as possible. Most firms in this day and age are stretched.

Maintenance

It's a fact of life: your web site is going to require maintenance. Just like you need someone to be in charge of the planning and implementation of the web site, you need someone to be in charge of the ongoing maintenance. When you are going through the planning process, you will need to decide what techniques for maintenance you are going to implement whether those are ezines or periodic updates to white papers. Once you decide what strategy you are going to use, then you will need to decide how often to update. Will you publish an ezine weekly, monthly or quarterly? How often will you publish articles?

Web sites can be set up so that someone in your firm can make the updates. However, I discourage this practice. Working with a professional is always best. Here's a funny story recently chronicled on Entreprenuer.com that proves this point.

A dentist was talking with his web designer, Tim Knox. The dentist asked the designer if he could show him how to update his own site, so he wouldn't have to pay anyone to have it done. The designer's coy reply? "Sure, I'll be glad, just as soon as you teach me how to clean my own teeth!" The point being, most people think there's nothing to web site maintenance. They believe they'll save some money by doing it themselves. What I normally find is, because this is usually not a task someone will do on a daily basis, the process of maintenance quickly becomes frustrating and the upkeep of the site slowly stops. Unless saving money is an absolute must, I recommend allowing your web design company to make updates and changes for you.

Budget

Yes, you will need to budget for your web site. I'm not going to try and put a number down for you because there are too many deciding factors that go into the cost of a site. Very simple ones can cost only a few hundred dollars. More complicated sites that include more bells and whistles can run in the tens of thousands. However, I will say this: the old adage "you get what you pay for" is still applicable today. You will also need to include an item in your budget for hosting the web site, monthly maintenance to the web site and search engine costs.

In an upcoming chapter on finding a web designer, I'll provide you with a worksheet, which includes questions to ask when collecting quotes.

7

Effective Design Elements for Professional-Looking Sites

"Design is a funny word. Some people think design means how it looks. But of course, if you dig deeper, it's really how it works."

Steve Jobs
Co-founder Apple

Three things can make or break your web site: the professionalism of your design, the information you choose to give visitors and the quality of your copy. If those three elements come together in harmony, your site stands a much better chance at accomplishing your goals than if one, two or all three elements are off-kilter.

It's important that we take a look at each of the three and make some notes, so you can effectively relate your thoughts to your designer. Let's look at the first two here, and we'll discuss copy in detail in a future chapter.

Professional Design Elements

When I ask new clients to list web sites that they find attractive, an inevitable response is, "I really can't think of any I like, but I sure can show you a lot of sites I don't like." Such is the curse of good design. Good design is invisible.

In the book, *Blink*, Malcolm Gladwell illustrates using neuroscience and psychological tests to show how people make snap judgments relying on the thinnest slices of experience and their unconscious. Many times people cannot articulate why they made a decision about something, but nonetheless they did make the decision regardless. If your web site is designed well, visitors will certainly notice. They may notice on a subconscious level, but they will take note.

Hire a Professional

Would you get your hair cut by a very young adult who has completed the first three months of beauty school, but not yet graduated? No! Why not? Because you have to look at yourself in the mirror every morning and you have to look your clients in the eye every day.

The same individuals who have their hair cut by unlicensed students who are only three months into their education are the ones who don't think twice about hiring a college student, high school student or Great Aunt Matilda's neighbor's son to design their web site.

The same applies to pre-made, web site templates. Buying a pre-made template may seem like a good idea upfront, but consider the following before making a decision:

- Web site templates are not search engine friendly. If ranking high in the engines is a priority for you (and it should be), templates are not the way to go.
- Making design changes to a template is often difficult and frustrating.
- Templates are sold to many companies meaning you and other CPAs could very easily end up with the same design.
- Pre-designed templates are not functional or customizable. If you plan to create a clients' area, templates are not recommended.

All that can be said is you get what you pay for. This will be the first impression many prospects get of your business. It may be the deciding factor for prospects you meet at networking events. Your site design will be a direct reflection on your firm, so it should be highly professional.

Showcase Your Business

Do you have a favorite restaurant? Perhaps it's a sophisticated place with excellent ambiance. You may not even know why you appreciate the atmosphere, but you do just the same. Was it the well-placed lighting, the tastefully chosen colors or the artwork on the wall? You focused on the food and have a definite opinion about that, but the environment may have escaped you. A web site with good design layout should be the same way. It lets the message be read loud and clear. Your visitor leaves with a positive feeling about your firm although they may have never truly paid attention to the specifics of the design.

Is Flashing Allowed?

Flash intros on a home page are not my idea of good design. These are the pages that consist of video-type moving pictures. (They get the name Flash from the type of software used to create them.) While many Flash intros can look wonderful, they generally don't accomplish the goals of the firm very well for several reasons:

Flash gets tedious after awhile. Visitors may be intrigued by your home page the first time or two they come to your site. After several visits, however, the Flash presentation gets monotonous.

Visitor preference is for non-Flash home pages. Many surveys have found that most visitors will skip Flash intros when they come to sites.

Search engines fumble with Flash. Search engines are text-based entities. That means they don't see graphics; they don't see images, and they don't see Flash. They only see and index words. Since Flash has no written content, the engines fumble when they reach pages consisting of all Flash.

Is there a place for Flash? Absolutely! You can use Flash on one section of your home page. You can make moving charts and graphs using Flash that are wonderfully descriptive. You can have Flash demonstrations or presentations on your site for new users or first-time visitors. Just don't make your entire home page Flash.

Since a picture is worth 1,000 words, let me show you some examples of home pages that really work.

Notice how the site does not have that much in graphics or artwork, yet it is very pleasing to the eye. The quality design allows the visitor to focus on the navigation and copy. The copy has good headlines and is chunked into sections, which we will discuss in detail a bit later. To a novice, this page may look very simple. Most effective designs are just that. That is the beauty of excellent web design. You focus on the information that is being presented, not the graphics.

Here's another one.

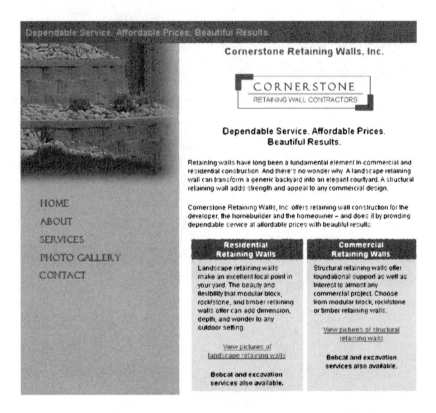

Notice how "clean" the design is? It's easy to read. The links are obvious and easy to find. The page is attractive, uses graphics well to add to the purpose of the site and incorporates elements that help the visitor decide how to navigate the site (segmenting residential and commercial customers). It leaves plenty of room for copy that explains the benefits of using this service.

This page does a wonderful job of visually representing the company, directing the visitor to the information s/he needs and encouraging interaction. The pictures of the giant, inflatable balloons the company makes quickly show the visitor what the site is all about. The navigation bar across the top provides direction plus the yellow search box helps visitors find examples of inflatables this company has created. Lastly, the ezine sign-up box gives the visitor an opportunity to interact with the company by becoming a subscriber.

This site does a phenomenal job of segmenting its audience. With general information in the main body copy, the visitor quickly gets an overview of what the site is about. Then, across the bottom of the page, five boxes offer direct links to pages with information specific to women, children, seniors, athletes and pets. What a great way to direct your prospects to information tailored just to them.

Open, visually interesting and easy to follow, this page captures the attention of site visitors plus leaves ample room for copy, so the message is obvious to those who visit.

Consistent Pages

Make sure that every page on your site looks like it is part of the overall web site. The graphics that you use on the top of your home page (such as your logo) should be on all the other pages of your site as well. It's confusing to visitors when the home page has one design and color scheme and the interior pages have a different design and color scheme. Many prospects will wonder if they've somehow left your site and clicked away to another company.

Effortless Navigation

What is navigation? Designers refer to the list of links that allow visitors to click to other pages of your site as the navigation bar. Here are two examples of navigation bars:

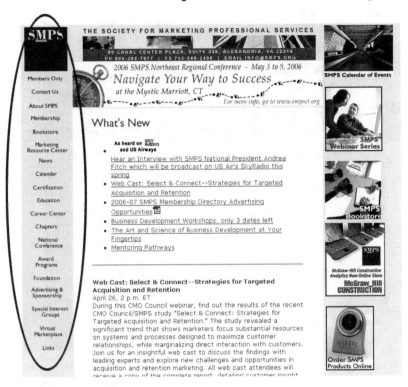

This site has a navigation bar down the left-hand sidebar. It clearly states what can be found by clicking each link.

Exquisite Flowers for Your Home or Business

Allegory specializes in sophisticated custom-designed creations:

- Fresh Flower Arrangements
- Silk and Dried Flower Arrangements
- Centerpieces and Individual Flower Designs
- Theme Decorations for Holidays and Special Occasions
- Floral Scene Setting for Photography
- Seasonal Decorations for the Home, Corporate Office or Restaurant

Flowers communicate – it's an idea as old as time. *Allegory* designs speak volumes about the care and thought you put into your business, home or event.

Allegory: Hyacinths represent wisdom, jasmine means grace, sunflowers stand for devotion and of course, roses for love. This is the allegory of flowers.

Serving Westchester, Fairfield, Putnam Counties, New York City.

Call today: 914.835.8233.

"I just wanted to thank you for the truly beautiful and unique floral arrangements you prepared for our Executive Headquarters. I would highly recommend your services to anyone looking for that special finishing touch."
Peggy Doepper
President and COO
Coldwell Banker Residential Brokerage

On the previous page, right across the top of the page, in plain sight, is the navigation bar. The names are very obvious: Home, Photo Gallery, Weddings, About, Resources, etc.

These links can also be repeated across the bottom of the page.

Navigation is the backbone of your web site. If the navigation is not strong, nothing else on the site can make up for it. The elements of strong navigation include:

- **Readable:** Your visitors should not have to hold their mouse over a link to be able to read it. Page names should be immediately obvious.

- **Intuitive:** Page names should make sense to visitors.

- **Repetitive:** Links to pages should appear on multiple areas of the web page.

- **Consistent:** The navigation bar should have the same page names and be in the same location(s) on every page of the site.

Have you ever visited a site and thought it only had a few pages? The navigation bar showed only two or three links? But, when you held your mouse over the link name, a menu with other pages dropped down. These are called (appropriately enough) "mouseover" links. While they have their limited purpose, they are not my recommendation for CPA web sites. Your navigation needs to be crystal clear. You have busy professionals visiting your site, and they don't have time to figure out the magical formula of how to navigate to the information they need. The fastest way for them to make it through your site is to have the navigation clearly laid out either on the top of the page or a sidebar (the left-hand or right-hand side sections of the screen).

The navigation should be intuitive. At this stage on the Internet, certain pages have become standard: home, about us and services are expected mainstays of any site. Visitors assume they will find these pages on practically every site. Clouding the navigation with cute little names such as "Your Best Options" instead of "Service" and "White & White Tells All" instead of "About Us" stretches creativity until it steps on the toes of functionality. This is not a time to be creative and think of new names for the standard pages.

Why repeat your navigation at the bottom of the web page? You want to help visitors more through your site as effortlessly as possible. You don't want any excuses for them to leave your site. Repeating links at the bottoms of pages makes your visitors' experience much more pleasurable because they don't have to keep scrolling from the top to the bottom to the top again.

Bottom page navigation is usually done in text, rather than graphic style. The navigation bar is also normally smaller than the primary one at the top of the page. You can see an example of a bottom page navigation bar below.

Home | Design | Services | Book | Ezine | About KLS | Contact

Copyright © 2006
KLS Web Solutions

Also, repeat navigation-page links within your copy. For example, when you write "contact us" on the home page, you can link directly to your Contact Us page. Your visitors do not have to hold that thought. They can act immediately. What a great thing for your business!

You already have a worksheet where you chose sites that you thought had a credible look and feel to them. Now you need to find sites with designs that appeal to you. It could be that some — or all — of the sites you listed before are visually appealing. If not, search for more sites to show your designer. As you list the sites, try to define what you like about each one. Likewise, find several sites that you don't like. Try to state what you don't care about for these sites.

Web Design Likes and Dislikes Worksheet

Find five web sites that you like and five web sites that you don't like. Try to explain what you do or do not like about each one.

Sites With Designs I Do Like

SITE ONE

www._____._____

What do you like about this site?

colors   graphics   navigation   font

layout   design elements   other:

_____

_____

_____

SITE TWO

www._____._____

What do you like about this site?

colors   graphics   navigation   font

layout   design elements   other:

_____

_____

_____

SITE THREE

www._____._____

What do you like about this site?

colors   graphics   navigation   font

layout   design elements   other:

_____

_____

_____

SITE FOUR

www._____._____

What do you like about this site?

colors   graphics   navigation   font

layout   design elements   other:

_____

_____

_____

SITE FIVE

www._____._____

What do you like about this site?

colors   graphics   navigation   font

layout   design elements   other:

_____

_____

Sites With Designs I Don't Like

SITE ONE

www._____._____

What don't you like about this site?

colors   graphics   navigation   font

layout   design elements   other:

_____
_____
_____

SITE TWO

www._____._____

What don't you like about this site?

colors   graphics   navigation   font

layout   design elements   other:

_____
_____
_____

SITE THREE

www._____._____

What don't you like about this site?

colors   graphics   navigation   font

layout   design elements   other:

_____
_____

SITE FOUR

www._____._____

What don't you like about this site?

colors   graphics   navigation   font

layout   design elements   other:

_____
_____
_____

SITE FIVE

www._____._____

What don't you like about this site?

colors   graphics   navigation   font

layout   design elements   other:

_____
_____
_____

_____

Your designer will appreciate any and all feedback you can give him/her, so try to be as complete as possible in your assessments of the sample sites.

NOTE: Visit www.KLSWebSolutions.com/Worksheets to print work-sheets from the Internet.

What Information to Include

How do you decide which pages to include on your site? There are some obvious ones, including the home page, services page, about us page and contact us page. But what else? We talked earlier about a clients' page to help show visitors the types of businesses or individuals you work with. Others to consider are:

- **Tax Updates:** Brief updates with information your clients need to be aware of.

- **Upcoming Events:** Does your firm sponsor workshops or seminars?

- **Forms:** Would you like to host various tax forms on your site for the convenience of your clients? You can!

- **Resources:** Another great idea is to have a page filled with online resources most individuals or businesses would need when dealing with accounting matters.

- **Ezine Archive:** If you choose to have an ezine, you could archive past issues on your site.

- **Testimonials:** We'll discuss this area in length in just a moment.

The list is virtually endless depending on what you want to provide to your visitors and clients. Give it some thought then — on the worksheet that follows — make a list of pages you think you would like to include.

Site Pages Worksheet

Which pages do you want to include on your web site?

Standard	Optional
❏ Home	❏ Clients
❏ Services	❏ Tax Updates
❏ About Us	❏ Upcoming Events
❏ Contact Us	❏ Forms
	❏ Resources
	❏ Ezine Archive
	❏ Testimonials

Other

List other pages you'd like to include and give a brief description of what information would be on the page(s). If you need additional space, make copies of this page or use notebook paper.

_____ : _____
_____

_____ : _____
_____

_____ : _____
_____

NOTE: Visit www.KLSWebSolutions.com/Worksheets to print worksheets from the Internet.

Testimonials

You work hard for your clients so let them give you a pat on the back. Then include those pats on your web site. Testimonials from your clients can be powerful marketing messages to visitors who come to your web site. However, testimonials need to be written properly to be the most effective. They need to be written to highlight the benefits your client received and to include the name of the person and company. Testimonials are wonderful for use on a testimonials page, but for maximum impact, you can also sprinkle them throughout your site — one or two on each page.

Highlight Benefits: As we've discussed before, visitors to your site are interested in "what's in it for me." They want to know you have solved problems similar to theirs. Therefore, testimonials from your current clients must demonstrate benefits by showing concrete, tangible results that your clients received from your work. For example, a testimonial that begins with, "Smith Partners cut our taxes by 10% after a review of . . ." will certainly pique a visitor's curiosity more than a testimonial that states, "We really liked working with Smith Partners. They always returned our calls promptly."

Don't think your clients can write testimonials like these? Not a problem! Most often, clients don't know what to say anyway. The best way I have found to handle this is to offer to write them for the clients. In fact, when I've asked clients to provide testimonials, they oftentimes request that I write it for them, and then allow them to edit it before it is used on my site. This kills two birds with one stone: your chances of getting a testimonial have increased tremendously, and the testimonial will be in the format you need, showing tangible results.

Sprinkle the Testimonials: Every visitor is different. The majority will never venture beyond your home page. The others that do will each choose their own paths if left to their own devices. That means they will wander from page to page with you not knowing who will go where. What you need to do to counteract this is give your full site some coverage in the area of testimonials. From my own client experience, it is rare that visitors click the testimonials page. For this reason, I recommend you sprinkle the testimonials throughout the web site and make sure your most powerful testimonial is on the home page. Your designer will have ideas about where to place testimonials on the page, so they contribute to each visitor's experience in the best way possible.

Name, Title and Company: One CPA client told me a particular visitor to her site chose to contact her because he personally knew one of the people who had given a testimonial to my client. It's a small world, and you never know who knows whom. For that reason, you should give as much information as possible about the person providing the testimonial: name, title and company. In addition, many people are jaded these days and are skeptical of testimonials that give initials only or that say something like, "Attorney, Denver, CO." Give as much information as your clients will be comfortable with. If they are willing to give their full name, excellent! Or if they will give a first initial and last name, use that. You might even ask if you can use their first name and last name initial. List their title, if they will let you and, at the very least, the name of the company with a link to the company's web site.

Describe the Company: One more simple but powerful way to make a testimonial really shine is to add a description of the company who provided it. For example, here is an ideal signature to a testimonial:

> John Doe, CFO
> Albeit Company
> Largest manufacturer of custom widgets in the northeast.

Ezine Sign-Up

I shouldn't tell you this because I'm a web designer, but I will anyway: the chances of someone visiting your site more than once are less than 5%. Do you ever think to yourself, *Oh, I better go back to that web site; they might have updated a page?* No, of course not, you are too busy and so is everyone else. Therefore, one of your site's goals is to capture your visitors' information, so you can keep in touch with them. If you're offering an ezine, you need to have an ezine sign-up **on the home page** because that's the place it will get seen most.

One client of mine gained 50 subscribers in three months from visitors that were looking for local services via the search engines. The subscribers came to the site and enjoyed reading previous issues that were made available on the site. They subscribed to my client's ezine and — from that point on — he was able to keep in touch with them via email. Now, 50 subscribers may not seem like many, but think about it — that's 50 people who would have likely never have returned to his site. Now, he's able to strike up a dialogue with them and potentially convert them to new clients.

An article written six months ago may hit a nerve with a visitor and cause him/her to contact you for services.

Because ezines are so very important, we will talk in-depth later on about the nuts and bolts of developing email campaigns to benefit your firm.

Give Away Value

When the very first web sites were launched over 20 years ago, they were long on information and short on design or functionality. There were no shopping carts or Flash intros. In fact, there was no e-commerce at all. The sites that existed were purely for information, sharing free content. This initial spirit of the Internet as a web of information continues in some form today. The vast majority of ezines are free of charge. They are a marketing tool that allows you to keep in touch with prospective clients and current clients.

As I've confessed to you — your site visitor probably isn't going to come to your site more than once. The best way to continue the relationship is with an ezine.

You might be concerned about people having too many emails in their inbox as it is. The beauty of ezines is that visitors choose to subscribe. They are, in essence, saying, "Please stay in touch with me. I want to receive your emails."

To get visitors to give away their email address, you might want to offer something free for each subscriber. Perhaps a free white paper like "10 Simple Ways to Cut Your Operating Costs by 10%." Visitors would probably be willing to give you their email address and try out your ezine in order to get information they need. Provided your ezine contains good, solid value, it is unlikely the person will unsubscribe. Now, you have a continuing relationship with a visitor you might otherwise never have seen again.

Keep in mind, people don't like the feeling of being sold. Your ezine should be a subtle selling tool that makes its points through proving your firm has exceptional knowledge and expertise. Directly selling to subscribers through your ezine will cause them to become wary. A study conducted by the CMO Council and KnowledgeStorm showed that 90% of business prospects who read research papers and case studies while visiting a web site said that those articles had a moderate to major impact on the process of narrowing down potential vendors. In addition 58% of prospects read them and then passed them along to colleagues and superiors. That gives you even more exposure.

8

What To Say and How To Say It: Proven Web Site & Search Engine Copywriting Practices

> "There is nothing to writing. All you do is
> sit down at a typewriter and open a vein."
> **Walter (Red) Smith**
> **American Sportswriter**

A s we mentioned in the previous chapter, good design is invisible. Subconsciously, people will decide that you are professional and reputable. The copy (text) on your site is far from invisible. To actually persuade visitors that they need your services you must have good, compelling copy. Also, to get good search engine rankings, you must have copy that is written to provide the engines with what they need to effectively assess, spider, index and rank your pages.

I know . . . most CPAs don't like to write. Especially if they must write marketing material such as web site copy. Thank goodness you don't have to! You can use any number of search engine copywriters to create text that will appeal to your target audience and give the engines what they need. Yes, this will add an additional amount to your budget. However, that investment will be one of the best you ever make. Professional copywriters are highly trained in connecting with your target audience and presenting information in a way that will be well received. This is a skill and talent not everyone has. I strongly encourage you to make the extra investment in professional copy, so your site will have optimal conversions.

So you will be familiar with what the copywriting process entails, and so you will have good information to provide to your copywriter, let's go over the basics of creating copy.

Before we begin, let me point out a major difference in reading from a paper document or book and reading from a lighted computer monitor from the Internet. An eye-tracking study conducted by the Poynter Institute in May 2000 of how people read articles on newspaper web sites reveals the following:

- 78% of the readers focused on text first.
- Readers preferred straightforward headlines.
- Readers read at only 75% of normal speed.
- Only 33% of the site visitors read a whole article.

What all this means is that most site visitors don't read much online. What they do read, they read more slowly. You have to compensate for that in your copy.

It's Not About You; It's About Them

I cannot implore you enough not to put copy on your site that is company-oriented. Copy should always be client-oriented. This is the #1 rule in professional copywriting. Your clients are the ones who have the money. They are the ones who will keep you in business. They are responsible for the success of your firm. The copy on your site should be written to, about and for them alone. Before I continue to jump up and down on my soapbox, let me take you back to the Target Audience Analysis you completed in an earlier chapter. This will be one of the most valuable documents you can provide to your copywriter.

The more your writer knows about your target customers, the more s/he will be able to connect with them through the copy. If you haven't done so already, fill out your Target Audience Analysis. If you rushed through it the first time, go back and provide just as much information as you possibly can.

Solving Problems

Part of the job of your copy is to solve the problems of your prospects. By addressing the issues they face and showing them your firm has the answers, you can quickly win over new clients. For example, let's say you often run into small business owners who struggle with doing their corporate quarterly tax returns. They get confused and frustrated and would really prefer that you handle that paperwork, but limited funds forces them to try to do as much work as they can on their own. If you choose to include a small business page on your site, you could easily solve this problem within your copy.

Perhaps your firm can do the first quarter's return each year as a guide, and then offer free telephone support for those who still have questions after looking over the work you've done. Your copy might read something like this:

> As a small business owner, you have more to do than you have hours in your day. While your aim is to save money by doing as much as you can yourself, it often leads to frustration and aggravation especially with quarterly tax returns. You'll find a solution when you follow a simple program we offer just for small business professionals.

Then you continue to explain how the offer works. See? You're not talking about you; you're talking to and about them. However, you've still managed to get the point across.

Are there other rules for writing effective copy? You bet! And you'll want to be aware of them, so you can know whether your copywriter has done his or her job well.

Let's look at some basics.

- **Capture your prospective client's attention with interesting headlines and sub-headlines.** This not only draws them in, but also keeps them moving through your text, so they can find out as much about you — and how you can help them — as possible. Which piques your sense of interest more: "Accounting Services in Denver" or "Accounting Services Customized for Small and Medium-Sized Organizations"? If you own a small or medium-sized business, the second headline is of more interest to you. Make the headlines interesting on your particular target client's level. Obviously, there is no need for headlines that scream obnoxious promises like "Accounting Services Designed to Skyrocket Your Profits and Pummel Your Tax Burden." But your headlines and sub-heads do need to spark curiosity or pique the interest of your site visitors to work well.

- **Condense information into bullet points.** Readers of both web sites and paper books are drawn to bullet points. I bet your eye was drawn to this section for that very reason. Bullets are a wonderful thing to include in your copy. There is no need to put all your copy into a bullet list (that would defeat the purpose), but including important points in bullet lists is a great way to capture attention.

- **Choose simple words to convey your message.** Did you know that most people read at or below a fifth-grade level? That's why most business publications are written at a fifth-grade reading level. The *New York Times* is actually an exception. This upscale newspaper is written at a sixth-grade level. The point is, you won't impress anyone with "superlative" language. Simple words work best every time.

- **Use shorter sentences.** As shown in the Poynter study earlier, people read differently on the web. Shorter sentences help them compensate for much of the distraction involved in reading from a lighted screen. Your sentences don't all need to be the same length; in fact, varying the length is best. Try to avoid sentences that run on unnecessarily. For example, look at the beginning of this bullet point. I could have said, "As shown in the Poynter study earlier, people read differently on the web; therefore, shorter sentences help them compensate for much of the distraction involved in reading from a lighted screen." Way too long! That's 31 words. Precisely why I broke that sentence up into two shorter sentences. While I won't set a specific word count to follow, I would encourage you to encourage your writer to look for ways to keep sentences as compact as possible.

- **Use short paragraphs.** Breaking up your text will improve the look of the page and will entice your site visitors to stay on your site longer. Most people are intimidated (or in dread) of long blocks of copy. Just the sight of it makes others want to click away. Let me show you. Take a look at the copy below.

When in the Course of human events it becomes necessary for one people to dissolve the political bands which have connected them with another and to assume among the powers of the earth, the separate and equal station to which the Laws of Nature and of Nature's God entitle them, a decent respect to the opinions of mankind requires that they should declare the causes which impel them to the separation. We hold these truths to be self-evident, that all men are created equal, that they are endowed by their Creator with certain unalienable Rights, that among these are Life, Liberty and the pursuit of Happiness. — That to secure these rights, Governments are instituted among Men, deriving their just powers from the consent of the governed, — That whenever any Form of Government becomes destructive of these ends, it is the Right of the People to alter or to abolish it, and to institute new Government, laying its foundation on such principles and organizing its powers in such form, as to them shall seem most likely to effect their Safety and Happiness. Prudence, indeed, will dictate that Governments long established should not be changed for light and transient causes; and accordingly all experience hath shewn that mankind are more disposed to suffer, while evils are sufferable than to right themselves by abolishing the forms to which they are accustomed. But when a long train of abuses and usurpations, pursuing invariably the same Object evinces a design to reduce them under absolute Despotism, it is their right, it is their duty, to throw off such Government, and to provide new Guards for their future security. — Such has been the patient sufferance of these Colonies; and such is now the necessity, which constrains them to alter their former Systems of Government. The history of the present King of Great Britain is a history of repeated injuries and usurpations, all having in direct object the establishment of an absolute Tyranny over these States. To prove this, let Facts be submitted to a candid world. He has refuted his Assent to Laws, the most wholesome and necessary for the public good. He has forbidden his Governors to pass Laws of immediate and pressing importance, unless suspended in their operation till his Assent should be obtained; and when so suspended, he has utterly neglected to attend to them.

Nobody likes the looks of a page like that. But what if we simply format it differently? It turns out to appear much more friendly. See?

When in the Course of human events it becomes necessary for one people to dissolve the political bands which have connected them with another and to assume among the powers of the earth, the separate and equal station to which the Laws of Nature and of Nature's God entitle them, a decent respect to the opinions of mankind requires that they should declare the causes which impel them to the separation.

We hold these truths to be self-evident, that all men are created equal, that they are endowed by their Creator with certain unalienable Rights, that among these are Life, Liberty and the pursuit of Happiness. — That to secure these rights, Governments are instituted among Men, deriving their just powers from the consent of the governed, — That whenever any Form of Government becomes destructive of these ends, it is the Right of the People to alter or to abolish it, and to institute new Government, laying its foundation on such principles and organizing its powers in such form, as to them shall seem most likely to effect their Safety and Happiness. Prudence, indeed, will dictate that Governments long established should not be changed for light and transient causes; and accordingly all experience hath shewn that mankind are more disposed to suffer, while evils are sufferable than to right themselves by abolishing the forms to which they are accustomed.

But when a long train of abuses and usurpations, pursuing invariably the same Object evinces a design to reduce them under absolute Despotism, it is their right, it is their duty, to throw off such Government, and to provide new Guards for their future security. — Such has been the patient sufferance of these Colonies; and such is now the necessity, which constrains them to alter their former Systems of Government. The history of the present King of Great Britain is a history of repeated injuries and usurpations, all having in direct object the establishment of an absolute Tyranny over these States. To prove this, let Facts be submitted to a candid world.

He has refuted his Assent to Laws, the most wholesome and necessary for the public good.

He has forbidden his Governors to pass Laws of immediate and pressing importance, unless suspended in their operation till his Assent should be obtained; and when so suspended, he has utterly neglected to attend to them.

Just shortening the paragraph lengths broke the copy up

enough to be inviting. Try to keep your paragraphs at three or four sentences in length, if you can.

Speak to Your Prospects

Words that you choose to convey your message are extremely powerful. Direct marketers (those who write marketing pieces delivered to your mailbox such as sales letters, postcards, flyers, etc.) have known this for years. Because they are famous as avid trackers, direct marketers have found some amazing facts pertaining to copywriting. For example, there are many examples of how changing just one word in a marketing headline can radically alter how successful the piece is for selling a product. Yes, just one word. John Caples, a legendary direct marketer, changed the word *repair* to the word *fix* in one mail piece and increased the response rate by 20%. Wow!

That's not an isolated event, either. Many of the best direct marketers have similar stories. They also have stories about effectively drafting copy that hits a nerve with the intended reader. You want your site visitors to feel welcomed at your site. You want them to know they've found a firm that understands them. You want prospects to feel comfortable approaching you. For those reasons, you need to speak to your visitors in their language. Using the following techniques will help.

- **Write conversationally.** A conversational style is easy to read, is inviting and makes the visitor feel comfortable. It will also keep your reader engaged.

- **Don't use jargon.** Make sure your prospective client understands your message with clear simple words. (Remember those reading levels!) Avoid accounting jargon at all costs when possible. Sure, sometimes there are no alternative words for what you need to say. But remember your visitors are not accountants. They don't know everything you know. And it's a good thing, too! If they knew everything you know, they wouldn't need you, now would they? Make it easy for them to understand what you're saying.

- **Use your clients' language.** This is one step beyond eliminating jargon. If you use your clients' language and not your own, you will increase their trust. They will pick up on the fact that you know them and understand where they are coming from. This is especially true for CPAs who have specialties. If you have a niche with real estate clients, you absolutely need to use real estate jargon in your copy. If you work primarily or exclusively with law firms, gear your copy toward legal terms. Any way you can let your visitor know you are in his/her corner, the better.

Provide Information

As we discussed previously, your site must cater to those who have the money to keep your firm in business. It's not about you; it's about them. While you may be tempted to have a lot of copy written that talks all about your firm, resist that temptation. Does all this sound familiar? It should. I don't mind repeating it, though. It bears repeating over and over again.

Your site should provide solid information that is helpful and useful to your visitors. This information can include:

- **Answers to Anticipated Questions:** Think about the questions your visitors are likely to ask. Go back to the Frequently Asked Questions page. Review the questions your customers most often have. Then incorporate some of those into your copy. The more intuitive the copy is, the more it is found valuable by the prospects, the better your conversion rate will be.

- **Features and Benefits:** In the DISC behavioral profile we discussed earlier in the book, you saw where the Steadiness type comprised 40% of the population. That group adores benefits. They aren't the only ones. The other groups do also. People want to not only see a list of services you offer, but to also know how — specifically — those services will benefit them in their own personal or professional life. To do this, you have to understand the difference between a feature and a benefit.

A feature is an attribute of the service. Electronic filing is fast. Fast is the feature. What is the benefit of having your return filed quickly? You get your refund sooner. Getting your refund sooner is the benefit. Don't give a feature without giving a benefit if you can help it. Rather than saying, "Electronic filing is available to help speed processing of your return" go one step further and say, "…so you get your refund sooner."

When writing with benefits, always ask yourself the question, "So what?" If you see your copywriter has included a list of services, read through the list and ask yourself, "So what?" Write the answers next to each feature, then send the list back to your copywriter and ask him/her to revise it to include the benefits that correspond with each feature.

- **Important Points Up Front:** There are several reasons to include the important points of each page up front. Many site visitors (I'd even venture to say most) read only a small percentage of the copy. The majority skim the text. So putting the important points first makes sense. It also makes sense if you're dealing with a target audience filled with either Dominance or Influence types (from the DISC model) or both. Neither is overly fond of details and won't read any more than they have to. But where on your site is "up front" exactly?

The most popular areas your customers will read include:

- headlines
- sub-headlines
- the first paragraph of the site
- the first sentence of other paragraphs
- bullet lists
- copy in shaded boxes
- captions for photos

If you have vital information, put it in one of these places to increase the probability it will get read.

- **Case Studies:** These are a great way to give prospects a view of the benefits that you have provided to clients. They are also a great way to showcase your services. Include as much detail as you legally can in order to take site visitors through every step of the process. The goal is to show them you know what you're doing, you know how to do it well, you have a track record for excellence and you're able to offer the services they need.

Search Engine Optimized Copywriting

If you want your site to rank highly in the search engines, you'll need to incorporate more than just web site copy. You'll need to make sure you have search engine optimized (SEO) copywriting. This specialty of copywriting involves focusing on the needs of your site visitor first, then also working in the most common elements that are known to help improve search engine ranking.

What you, as a CPA, need to know is how to determine if the SEO copy is any good or not. You also need to be aware of the best and worst practice in this specialty. In addition, you'll want to be aware of what good and bad SEO copy is and what questions to ask an SEO copywriter to ensure s/he will do a good job.

Worst Practices in SEO Copywriting

Unfortunately, the field of SEO copywriting has begun to get flooded with those who say they know how to write effective SEO copy when, in fact, all they do is stuff keywords everywhere they could possibly fit. (Remember, keywords and keyphrases are the actual search terms visitors type into search engines to try to find what they are looking for. "CPA" might be a keyword and "corporate CPA services" might be a keyphrase.) The copy should make sense when you read it. The copy should not sound like a forced, regurgitated bundle of keywords and phrases that are simply repeated over and over.

Here are some things you definitely want to avoid when it comes to SEO copywriting:

Do Not Replace Every Generic Phrase With a Keyphrase

This is one of the most common bad practices in SEO copywriting. Many so-called SEO copywriters will simply take the information you provide to them, then will replace every instance of "tax accounting" (for example) with "Atlanta tax accounting services." They replace a generic term with a keyphrase. The problem with this practice is that it never sounds right. Let me give you an example.

> White & White, CPA provides expert small business Atlanta tax accounting services along with retirement planning, merger and acquisition services and more. If you're looking for an Atlanta tax accounting services firm, be sure to contact us about your Atlanta tax accounting services needs.

No, unfortunately, I'm not kidding. Do not let an SEO copywriter tell you this is the way your copy has to sound if you want to rank high on the search engines. It most certainly does not have to sound like a ridiculous bundle of junk.

Don't Use "The List"

Another distasteful practice amateur SEO copywriters use is "the list." They will list every one of your keyphrases consecutively each time they can find an opportunity. Now, granted, there may be an occasional instance when listing all the keyphrases is appropriate, but this practice should not be used repeatedly through a page. For instance, if your chosen keyphrases are: "Atlanta tax accounting," "merger and acquisition services Atlanta" and "CPA retirement planning," you would not want your copy to read as follows:

> We provide Atlanta tax accounting, merger and acquisition services Atlanta and CPA retirement planning plus a variety of other services you will need throughout the year. Search the Internet and you will quickly find that we are the primary source for quality Atlanta tax accounting, merger and acquisition services Atlanta and CPA retirement planning services.

This practice and the "replace" practice above it are only used by elementary SEO copywriters or editors who don't have the skills to create copy that sounds logical and also meets the needed criteria for the engines. Do not work with a copywriter who shows you samples that contain these two tactics.

What are other bad practices? Here are two more to be wary of.

Creating Content Solely for the Engines

Your content should provide value for your site visitors, period! Many SEO companies and/or copywriters will advise you to create pages that have the sole purpose of attracting the search engines. This is never a good idea. The pages often sound worse than the examples above, and they bring no credibility to your site.

You'll hear reasoning including "These are high traffic search terms and if you don't optimize pages for them, you'll lose tons of business." Ignore their pleas. You'll lose even more business if those thousands of supposed visitors come to your site and find copy that is appallingly lacking in information or help.

Keywords Should Always Fit the Page

Another shaky tactic is to attempt to use keyphrases on pages where they simply don't fit. This, too, is done to appease the search engines and — like all the other practices — is never a good idea.

For example, if you were to have a page dedicated to small businesses, you would not want to include keyphrases such as "corporate tax accounting." It simply wouldn't make sense. Beware of those who assure you, "We'll find a way to fit it in, so you can benefit from all that extra traffic." Famous last words!

So what should you do? What are the good practices in SEO copywriting? There are several to keep in mind.

Always Research Keywords and Phrases

Never guess about the search terms people are typing into Google and the other engines. There's no reason to guess. There are many valid services available online that can quickly show you exactly which words and phrases have been searched on that apply to your firm. If your copywriter asks you to guess to save a little time and money, fire your copywriter!

Ask to see the research results. Don't be satisfied with a list of keywords or phrases from your search engine optimizer or copywriter. (Keyword research is normally a function of an SEO company, but occasionally copywriters have been known to do keyword research.) They should be able to provide you with the competition levels, the expected number of searches per month and the current traffic levels for that keyword/phrase.

Generally speaking, you'll want to use keyphrases, not singular keywords. In the early days of the Internet, surfers would type in singular words such as "marketing" or "Lexus" or whatnot. There was very little competition back then, so single word searches were common and produced fairly accurate results. However, as the Internet grew and thousands of sites turned into millions of sites, surfers began to notice that a search for "chairs" brought up extremely diverse results, including everything from chair repair to reclining chairs to folding chairs to antique chair restoration and so forth. Searchers began to narrow their focuses by broadening their search strings.

Now, instead of searching for single word keywords like "chairs," searchers are typing in more sophisticated search strings like "swivel rocker reclining chair." They've learned that the more specific their search string is, the more accurate their results will be. This is why you don't want to target single keywords like "CPA" or "taxes" or whatnot. You want multi-word keyphrases like "Denver CPA" or "small business tax accounting" and the like. (All these keywords and phrases I've listed are just examples. I have not researched any of them, so please don't assume they are viable terms for your copy.)

If you want to research keyphrases on your own, or if you want to see what tools professionals use, you can visit:

www.wordtracker.com

www.keyworddiscovery.com

I do not recommend using the Overture (now Yahoo!) keyword research tool. It is lacking in many areas and gives unreliable results. For instance, this tool combines the singular and plural versions of keywords and phrases. It also combines any other variations such as "ing," "est" and so on. Therefore, if you were researching possible keyphrases using the term "New Year's Eve event," Overture/Yahoo! would combine all the versions of "New Year's Eve event" and "New Year's Eve events." You would have no way of knowing whether to use the singular version or the plural version. Most often, the plural versions of keyphrases get much higher results, but you never want to guess. You need to know for sure.

Keyphrases Should Be Virtually Unnoticeable

When all is said and done, you should barely be able to detect the keyphrases in the copy. Let me show you some SEO copy that is well written. Can you pick out what the keyphrases are? Three different keyphrases were used. See if you can find them.

Exceptional Finds in Center City
Philadelphia Real Estate for Sale

The Center City real estate marketplace is bustling with people who love to be in the middle of it all. With an extensive variety in home styles and numerous centrally located businesses, downtown Philadelphia has the unique advantage of offering a little of everything. Just imagine stepping out your door and strolling

---

leisurely down cobblestone streets as you make your way to work or shopping in Center City Philadelphia. Real estate for sale in this area means you'll likely get a glimpse of Fairmount Park — the largest landscaped inner city park in America — that runs throughout South Philadelphia.

Each area of the Center City real estate market highlights something special for those who wish to live in downtown Philadelphia. Society Hill homes offer picturesque 17th and 18th century designs graced with tree-lined streets as well as contemporary townhomes amid museums, theaters, restaurants, and boutique shops. Within walking distance of practically everything you might want in south Philadelphia, Society Hill homes flawlessly combine peace and tranquility with the heartbeat of the city.

Well? Could you find them? The keyphrases are:

- Center City Philadelphia Real Estate
- Center City Real Estate
- Philadelphia Society Hill Homes

Here's where they are in the copy:

Exceptional Finds in Center City Philadelphia Real Estate for Sale

The Center City real estate marketplace is bustling with people who love to be in the middle of it all. With an extensive variety in home styles and numerous centrally located businesses, downtown Philadelphia has the unique advantage of offering a little of everything. Just imagine stepping out your door and strolling leisurely down cobblestone streets as you make your way to work or shopping in Center City Philadelphia. Real estate for sale in this area means you'll likely get a glimpse of Fairmount Park — the largest landscaped inner city park in America — that runs throughout South Philadelphia.

Each area of the Center City real estate market highlights something special for those who wish to live in downtown Philadelphia. Society Hill homes offer picturesque 17th and 18th century designs graced with tree-lined streets as well as contemporary townhomes amid museums, theaters, restaurants, and boutique shops. Within walking distance of practically everything you might want in south Philadelphia, Society Hill homes flawlessly combine peace and tranquility with the heartbeat of the city.

See? The keyphrases don't have to be clumped together in a list. They don't have to awkwardly replace the generic terms in the copy. They don't have to stand out like a sore thumb. Here's another example. Let's do the same test. See if you can find the one keyphrase used in this copy.

**Book Your Exotic Cruise Vacation Online
and Get Rock-Bottom Prices to the Hottest Destinations**

Just imagine . . . you're walking along the deck of a grand cruise vessel as it gently keeps rhythm with the waves. The sun is on your shoulders and a soothing breeze wafts through your hair. You're in the middle of an exotic cruise vacation heading for your next port of call. Your every need is attended to by cruise vacation professionals whose job it is to make sure you are completely relaxed, stress-free and happy.

This can all be yours! You can take vacations on major cruise lines to the most exciting destinations when you book your cruise online with Cruise Vacation Center.

What's the keyphrase? "Cruise vacation." It makes sense on the page. It fits with the copy. It flows naturally, so it doesn't stand out at all.

Hiring a Copywriter

What questions should you ask when hiring a copywriter? You'll find a list on the next page that will help you weed out the amateurs from the pros. You'll also find a checklist you can use to evaluate the copy once it has been written to be sure it will meet your goals.

Questions for Copywriter Interviews

1. How long have you been writing web copy? _____

2. How long have you been writing SEO copy? _____

3. What types of clients have you written for? _____
_____
_____

4. Do you have specific experience in writing for CPAs?_____
_____

5. Can you send me (or show me online) samples of your work for a variety of clients—SEO and non-SEO? _____
_____

6. Can you send me (or show me online) samples of your work for CPAs — SEO and non-SEO? _____
_____

7. Do you have references I can call?_____
_____
_____
_____

8. Do you perform keyword research or do I need to provide keywords and phrases for use in the copy? _____
_____

9. How many keyphrases do you normally include in a page of copy? _____

10. What length do you consider to be one page of copy? (How many words?) _____

11. How do you charge? (By the page, by the hour, by the project?) _____

12. What are your rates for SEO and non-SEO copy? _____

_____

_____

_____

13. How many revisions are included? _____

14. What is your charge for edits or changes over and above that number of revisions? _____

15. What do you require from me to get started? (Tell him/her you have a target audience analysis you can provide.) _____

_____

_____

_____

_____

16. When are you available to start? _____

17. How long will it take to complete the copy once you begin? ___

_____

If you need additional space, make copies of this worksheet or use notebook paper.

NOTE: Visit www.KLSWebSolutions.com/Worksheets to print work-sheets from the Internet.

Checklist for SEO Web Site Copy

After you receive the copy from the copywriter, check it against this list. This is a good review for copy designed to persuade visitors to hire you. This checklist would not be appropriate for other types of pages such as About Us, Testimonials, Contact Us, member-only pages, etc.

Does/Is the copy:

_____ client-focused, not company-focused?

_____ show how your firm solves visitors' problems?

_____ include interesting headlines and sub-headlines?

_____ use bullet lists when appropriate?

_____ use simple words?

_____ have shorter sentences?

_____ include shorter paragraphs?

_____ conversational?

_____ avoid CPA industry jargon?

_____ use language/terms appropriate to the clients' industries?

_____ answer anticipated questions?

_____ provide features and benefits?

_____ feature important points up front (including in headlines, sub-headlines, first paragraph, first sentence of other paragraphs, bullet lists, shaded boxes, photo captions, etc.)?

_____ offer case studies?

Does SEO copy:

_____ avoid "the replace" and "the list" tactics?

_____ offer content valuable to the visitor and the search engine?

_____ make use of keywords and keyphrases that fit the page?

_____ use keywords and phrases that have been researched, not guessed about?

_____ have keywords that flow and are virtually unnoticeable within the copy?

If you need additional space, make copies of this worksheet or use notebook paper.

NOTE: Visit www.KLSWebSolutions.com/Worksheets to print worksheets from the Internet.

9

Search Engines: Are They Worth It?

"There is far more opportunity than there is ability."
Thomas Edison
Inventor and Businessman

Bringing thousands of new potential clients to your door who are looking for your services is a definite benefit your firm can enjoy from the Internet. One of the key ways people find your web site is through the search engines.

Let's start at the very beginning and discuss the nuts and bolts of search engines.

Search Engines

As I write this, there are primarily three search engines used by the public: Google, MSN and Yahoo!. These search engines — using a complex secret mathematical formula (algorithm) to determine the importance of each page (relevance) — review (spider) the many web pages that are published on the Internet. The information they consider to be the most relevant is included in the engine's different datacenters.

When someone visits Google and enters a search term (keyword) into the search box, the search engine will retrieve web pages containing those words and list the pages in order of importance based on the engine's latest algorithms.

Do you have a migraine yet? Hold on. Don't take that aspirin just yet. We have more to cover.

Spiders

The United Nations Conference on Trade and Development released information confirming that over 10.7 million new web sites are added to the Internet every year. I don't even want to guess how many sites are indexed by Google. Suffice it to say the number is in the **billions** and continues to grow daily. How did all these sites get into the search engines' datacenters?

Search engine spiders (also referred to as bots, derived from the term robots) are actually programs that travel through the Internet looking for new web pages or updated web pages. When they find some, they are programmed to evaluate the page to determine what subject matter it addresses, if it has relevant material of high quality and about 1,000 other things. When the spider finds such pages, it alerts the datacenter and the page is indexed.

Once the page is indexed (that is, it is included somewhere in the search engine's datacenter, but not necessarily up top), the next step is to rank the page. Ranking consists of the engine comparing the page to its algorithm to see how the content, coding, linking and other aspects line up with what the engine is looking for. If the page lines up well with the engine's criteria, your page will be ranked highly. If the page does not line up well, it will be ranked low on the totem pole.

The famous line, from the movie, *Field of Dreams*, "If you build it, they will come" is certainly not true for your web site. You must keep in mind that your firm's web site — in and of itself — will not automatically attract lots of visitors. It takes planning and work to purposely cause your site to rank highly with the search engines. While no one knows exactly what is contained in the engines' various algorithms, there is a good deal of knowledge about what helps get pages ranked highly and what does not. Let's talk about that for a bit, so you can have a working understanding of the process and what to expect from it.

Behind the scenes, your designer will be creating your site using a type of coding language such as HTML, ASP, PHP, etc. This is what actually makes your site look the way it does and perform the functions you want it to perform. Want to see it? You can! Go to any web site you choose. It doesn't matter which one. Once you're there, look at the top of your browser screen and click "View." Then, on the drop-down menu, click "Source." A little window with a bunch of junk will pop up. That's your source code! All that jumbled bunch of nonsense is what makes your site run.

The coding of your site will have a big impact on whether your site is spidered by the search engines. Think of the coding as Braille and the search engine spiders as fingers "reading" the Braille. If your site is coded well, the search engine will glide through your site, quickly reading the information. The spider will see both information that appears to the public and also information that appears only in your code. The spider will also easily navigate from your home page to the other pages on your site in order to possibly index this information.

Notice we are talking about individual pages at this point. Spiders travel from page to page (via links on other sites that point to pages on your site and also via links on your site that point to individual pages within your site's structure) to collect information. Your entire site is not spidered, indexed or ranked as a whole. Each page must stand on its own merits.

Unfortunately, many web sites are so poorly coded that the spider can't get any information from them. For instance, if the code is unorganized or jumbled, it can stump the spiders leaving them confused about the page. If the page contains JavaScript (an applet that allows certain functions to work such as pop-up windows, etc.) and that script is not well organized or not contained within its own area, the spiders can miss important information in the code. Extensive Flash presentations (moving pictures) on pages can have the potential to cause the spiders to see absolutely nothing when they try to read the code.

If the navigation of your site isn't clean (that is, well thought out so that each page has at least one link to it), the spiders can get lost and not find every page on your site. It can truly lead to a messy situation that prevents your site from reaching its ultimate goals when it comes to search engine optimization.

Firms are mistakenly led to believe that their web pages will automatically appear in the search engines. This is not the case. At a minimum, your site needs to have good, clean coding, so the engines can read every page of your site. This will help you with having every opportunity to appear high in the search results when someone types in a keyword or keyphrase related to your company.

And what if you don't want a particular page (or pages) to appear in the search engines? You can easily exclude those pages via a special tag. This way, password-protected client-only areas or other sections containing highly sensitive information will not be revealed to the engines or made public through the search engine results pages. This tag is included in your source code.

How can you avoid problems with messy code? There are several things you can do.

The Importance of Linking

Just how do these spiders find your site to begin with? Through links. Contrary to popular belief, it is not necessary to submit your site to the search engines unless it is a first-time site that has just recently been uploaded to the Internet. If you have an existing site, the spiders will automatically find you through the links that point to it.

While the engines are changing their algos constantly, currently a linking strategy is an integral part of any SEO program. Make sure your SEO firm offers link-building (also called link popularity) campaigns and that they conduct them ethically.

Link popularity is calculated by the search engines based on how many web sites are linking to your site. Very simply stated, the more sites that link to your site, the more "popular" (and relevant) the search engines believe your site is. The links coming from your site (directing to other sites) will discount this popularity. Therefore, you want to attract as many sites as you can to link into your site — preferably without having to provide a reciprocal link back to them.

A word of caution must be made: there are many companies out there that will promise to quickly (read: overnight) provide thousands of links to your site for a fee. These companies have been termed "link farms," and the search engines do not approve of them. If a search engine tracks links to your site and finds them coming from a link farm, the search engine will drop your site from their index like a hot potato. This is a highly unethical practice. Once your site has been dropped from a search engine, it is very difficult for it to be reinstated. Stay away from link farms!

What should you be doing to gain reputable links? Good practices with link building include:

> 1. Providing valuable information on your site, so other sites will naturally want to link to you.

> 2. Registering with Yahoo!, DMOZ and specialty directories as these create powerful one-way links to your site.

> 3. Submitting articles to free article distribution sites. Your "bio" at the end of each article will contain a link back to your site.

Reciprocal links are not as powerful as one-way links for SEO purposes, but can bring very qualified traffic to your site. For that reason, reciprocal links should not be discounted.

> 1. Trade links with sites that are from non-competing, complimentary businesses. These could include lawyers, financial planners, bookkeepers, etc.

> 2. Include links pointing to other sites on a "Resources" or "Helpful Sites" page rather than your "Home" page.

> 3. Links to other sites should open in another browser window, so visitors to your site will not lose their place. When they are ready to continue reading your information, their original browser window will still be open.

Avoiding Messy Code

"Clean code" is a very important term you want to remember. You always want every page of your site to have clean code. This means that — regardless of the language your site was built using (HTML, ASP, PHP, XML, CSS, etc.) — the code is free of extraneous, garbled symbols and scripts that can get in the way of the spiders having free access to roam and index at will. To keep things in line, most designers abide by these rules of thumb:

1) Don't use WYSIWYG editors.

WYSIWYG stands for "what you see is what you get." This term is pronounced "wiss-e-wig." These are programs that allow you (or your designer) to create web pages using images and words rather than just strings of code. The WYSIWYG programs develop the code as you add words and images to each web page. However, design programs like FrontPage or GoLive are notorious for leaving behind extraneous code. It's better that your designer knows how to hand code all web pages if needed. If your designer is using one of these (or similar) programs, be sure s/he understands how to evaluate the code to make sure it is clean.

2) Use call files for scripts.

Scripts of almost any type (Java, Flash, etc.) can cause what is referred to as "bloated code." This means there is just way too much code on the page for a spider to effectively wade through. To keep the code clean, designers can remove the sections of code that pertain to scripts and put it in its own private space referred to as a "call file."

In place of the bloated script code, the designer will insert one simple line of code that points to the new call file. When a spider comes along, it will read the call line and understand the page contains Java or Flash or another type of complicated script, but will not have to sort through the enormous amount of complex code that is irrelevant to your site's rankings.

Here is an example of a call file that could appear in your site's code:

```
<script language="JavaScript" type="text/JavaScript" src="scripts/
rollover.js">
</script>
```

Rather than the entire JavaScript file being listed in the code itself, a "scripts/rollover.js " call tag was created that pulls the JavaScript code from another source. This helps to keep the code clean and easily spiderable.

3) Separate sections of code.

Another way to keep your source code clean is to have your designer separate the different sections with a few blank lines. For instance, the top section of your page's code is referred to as the "header" section. The next section might include some images, a table and a small Flash presentation. You can encourage your designer to insert blank lines between each section to make them easier to find. See the example below.

```
<!DOCTYPE HTML PUBLIC "-//W3C//DTD HTML 4.01 Transition-
al//EN" "http://www.w3.org/TR/html4/loose.dtd">
<html>
```

NOTE THE BLANK LINES BETWEEN THE INTRODUCTION AND THE HEADER SECTION.

```
<head>
<TITLE>new york web design - web design westchester - html web-
page designs</TITLE>
<META NAME="description" CONTENT="Mustang, a new york
web design firm, will generate business for you while you sleep!
Create a web site that really works for you. Visit today.">
<META NAME="keywords" CONTENT="new york web design,
ecommerce, webpage design, NYC web design, internet market-
ing, ecommerce for small business, web site designers, web site
marketing">
<meta        http-equiv="Content-Type"        content="text/html;
charset=iso-8859-1">
<LINK REL="stylesheet" HREF="css/mustangcss.css" TYPE="text/
css">
</head>
```

NOTE THE BLANK LINES BETWEEN THE HEADER SECTION AND THE BODY.

```
<body>
<table width="85%" border="0" align="center" cellpadding="5"
cellspacing="0" bgcolor="#FFFFFF">
<tr>
    <td><a href="newyorkwebdesign.htm"><img src="images/
weblogomustang.gif" alt="Mustang, a new york web design firm,
helps small professional firms create sites that work!" width="92"
height="100" border="0"></a></td>
</tr>
<tr>
    <td><img src="images/tagline2mustang.gif" width="331"
height="12" alt="Harness the power of the internet for your
firm."></td>
</tr>
<tr>
    <td align="center" class="color"><a href="index.htm">Home</
a>  | 
    <a href="client.htm">Client Portfolio</a> |  <a
href="service.htm">Services</a>
    |  <a href="about.htm">About Us</a> |  <a
href="contact.htm">Contact Us</a>
    |  <a href="guide.htm">Free Resources</a> </
td></tr>
</table>
```

NOTE THE BLANK LINES BETWEEN THE BODY AND THE FIRST TABLE.

```
<table width="85%" border="0" align="center" cellpadding="10"
cellspacing="0" bgcolor="#FFFFFF">
<tr>
    <td colspan="3" class="bgtable"><H1>Home</H1>
    <p class="quote">&#8220;Kristi has a solid understanding of
website design.
```

Simplicity of the design process, understanding my objectives and her

willingness to work through technical difficulties were just a few things

I really appreciated about Kristi. My new site accurately represents

my business and puts me at ease about sending prospects and
clients to
view it.”
<span class="quote2">Howard E. Greenberg
President,
Howard Properties, LTD.
Recipient of several awards granted by the Mack-Cali
Broker Hall of Fame</span></p>
</td>
</tr>
<tr>
<td width="40%" valign="top">

NOTE THE BLANK LINES BETWEEN THE FIRST TABLE AND THE SECOND TABLE.

You get the idea.

To be sure your code stays clean, your designer can validate it at
these sites:

Free Evaluation Version of HTML Validator

www.htmlvalidator.com

W3C Free Code Validator

www.validator.w3.org

W3C Free Code Validator for other languages (CSS, XHT-ML, XML)

www.w3schools.com/site/site_validate.asp

So, what about the algorithms I mentioned earlier? What about
the mystery programs that search engines judge your site's pages
against? How important are they and what do you need to know
about them?

Algorithms

To determine the relevance of your site, search engines use algorithms. As I mentioned earlier, these are "secret" formulas that the search engines use to determine the ranking of your site in the search engines. The battle for the engine that returns the most relevant results is fierce. Millions of dollars are at stake, so, naturally, every engine keeps its algorithm (sometimes called an "algo" for short) under wraps. The search engines' goals are to deliver a list of quality web sites to people who are searching based on the search terms that were typed in. You may not have known there was so much behind the inner workings of a search engine. It's not like your local Yellow Pages where every site is automatically included.

Search engines strive to provide very relevant results. When you go to Google, for example, and type in "dog collars," the list of search results that come up have been filtered repeatedly to try and make them as accurate as possible. Google (and others) want to make sure you're getting results that actually pertain to dog collars and not dogs in general, dog food, dog kennels, dog supplies, etc. The behind-the-scenes effort it takes to actually make that happen is enormous.

Because they continually strive to make their results increasingly relevant, the search engines will change and tweak their algorithms. This is also in an attempt to eliminate people from trying to trick the search engines into listing their pages when they aren't relevant. When an algo changes (called an update), many sites are found floundering in the rankings. However, those who use proven, aboveboard search engine optimization (SEO) practices normally fair very well. Their rankings may fluctuate some, but generally they will rebound within a short time.

Search Engine Optimization

How do we know all that we know about spiders and algos? Through the art and science of search engine optimization. Yes, there is an entire industry built around trying to discover what the engines are after, then giving it to them. This is big business. Although the search engines use secret formulas to rank web pages, an entire industry has evolved in studying web sites and how to improve their rankings.

Just as the algorithms change (or maybe I should say "because" the algos change), many of the strategies for achieving high rankings change. However, many of the foundational aspects of SEO are still in place. Let's look at what's old news and what's considered current events in the area of SEO.

META Tags

META tags are a part of your source code. They are placed near the top and include several types of tags that give information to spiders about different aspects of the page. The most recognized tags are these:

> **META Keywords Tag**: The keywords and key-phrases you hope to rank highly for can be placed in this tag.

> **META Description Tag**: A short description of the page is placed here.

> **META Title Tag**: The title of the page goes in this tag.

About four years ago, keyword META tags were incredibly important. Webmasters would spend hours, if not days, coming up with the search terms to include in this tag. That was really all you had to do to rank high in the engines... put a lot of keywords into the tag. What began to happen was that sites with little to no relevance to particular phrases were putting arbitrary keywords into their tags. Soon, the engines picked up on this scam and changed their algos. Sites that were using irrelevant keywords suddenly found themselves dropped from the rankings. Now, this tag is basically obsolete and ignored by the search engine spiders. It won't hurt to put your keywords into this tag, but it isn't necessary any longer. Sites that were using only terms that truly did apply to their sites got shuffled around a bit, but soon landed in the same — or a higher — position than before.

The description tag has always had a fair amount of importance. This will sometimes show on the search results page. Sometimes, engines will pull a snippet of copy from your page to use instead of the description tag. Nonetheless, you need to develop a strong description tag for the times that it is used. The tag should be written with a good level of customer appeal. After all, it will be partially responsible for enticing searchers to click over to your site.

The title tag has always held an important place in the SEO world. Currently, it has elevated in importance as the engines are placing more weight on it. One reason the title tag is so vital is that the title tag is the first thing a searcher will see in relation to your site. When the search results page shows up, the bold, underlined title tags are what get the command attention. Look at the following screenshot. This is from Google's search results page for the phrase "Hilton Head attractions."

The title tag is circled above. Do you see that each page has its own title tag? Because the keywords are shown in bold, the title tag catches your eye first. That's why your title tags should always be enticing and give good information. So, what types of attractions are we looking to find on Hilton Head Island? As you can see, the title tags above give us clues as to what's available: things to do, museums, festivals and so on. From there, we read the description to get more information and decide if we want to click over to the site for a look. So, you see, some META tags are not only for search engine use, but also for visitor use.

Oftentimes, but not always, copywriters create the META tags. You can add that question to your Copywriter Interview worksheet if you'd like. Most frequently, the search engine optimizer will develop tags for you. Below is an example of what the META tags actually look like in your site's code.

```
<TITLE>new york web design - web design westchester
- html webpage designs</TITLE>
<META NAME="description" CONTENT="Mustang, a new
york web design firm, will generate business for you
while you sleep! Create a web site that really works
for you. Visit today.">
<META NAME="keywords" CONTENT="new york web design,
ecommerce, webpage design, NYC web design, internet
marketing, ecommerce for small business, web site
designers, web site marketing">
```

So, the elements of search engine optimization (SEO) that are important include research, implementing the strategy and continually reviewing the strategy.

Research

Research is the first step in performing search engine optimization. **This step is crucial!** Keyphrases are the very heart and sole of search engine optimization. It's where everything starts. If you target the wrong keyphrases, all your other efforts will reap small rewards, if any. The whole point of SEO is to get your site in front of those who are searching for you. In order to do that, optimizers have to know what words and phrases searchers are inputting into the engine's search field. They then take those words/phrases and optimize your pages using the information they've researched in an effort to get your pages ranked highly.

When performing SEO for a client, optimizers usually ask the client to very quickly write down words that they believe would be used to find their services if someone searched for them on a search engine. This initial step should be done quickly without a lot of time thinking about details. It is a short exercise to help the optimizer begin the keyword research process.

The next step is to get cold hard facts and figures to verify which phrases will bring about good results and which will not. Most optimizers use a software program that will tell how popular a particular search term is and how many sites are optimizing for this phrase. As mentioned in the chapter on copywriting, the two most popular tools include:

www.wordtracker.com

www.keyworddiscovery.com

Let's look at the information an optimizer might find if conducting research on Wordtracker for the term "certified public accountant michigan."

This is what you see on the results page of Wordtracker.

As you can see, not only does the original keyphrase show up, but also alternatives that you might want to consider are given.

The phrase we searched on is showing a total of fifty searches predicted per day. The next term shown is "Employment certified accountant michigan." That term is simply not usable. Quite frankly, sometimes people type odd phrases into search engines and this is the result. These junk terms cannot be used as-is for good results within your copy.

Let's move on to the next step in the process . . . finding out the levels of competition. The next screenshot will show the information given by Wordtracker.

"Certified public accountant michigan" has 260 sites competing for rankings. The number 39 in the "popularity" column gives the estimated search traffic within 24 hours for one search engine only. (The previous "predicted" amount was for all search engines.) This is the type of data you and your web site team need in order to develop an effective design, copywriting and SEO strategy.

The researcher would repeat this process with each term on your initial list. S/he would then begin to combine terms and research alternatives that might be used with good results. In the end, you should be provided with a list that includes the recommended search terms, the predicted traffic levels and the amount of competition for each term.

NOTE: The Internet is an ever-changing environment, and keyphrase popularity is altered almost daily. When conducting your own keyphrase research, your results will most likely vary.

SEO Implementation

Once the keywords have been determined, the web site will be optimized for these words. Here the web designer or SEO will make the appropriate changes to the coding and design elements. The copywriter will handle optimizing the copy as discussed in the previous chapter.

When overseeing your SEO-friendly design, watch for these dos and don'ts.

- **Don't use frames**. Frames is the name of a particular web page layout. Currently, search engine spiders can potentially have difficulty navigating sites designed with frames. As search engines continue to improve, this may not always be the case, but for now, avoiding frames is best.

- **Don't use all Flash**. As previously mentioned, Flash movies contain no readable text that the search engine can spider. While you can have small Flash presentations on your site, creating entire pages designed in Flash is not a good idea if achieving high rankings is your goal.

- **Don't use extensive amounts of Java**. If Java is needed on your site, use it sparingly and — when possible — have your designer use call files to avoid cluttered code.

- **Do have a reasonable amount of copy**. In a perfect world, having about 250-400 words of copy on your pages is the way to go. This, however, also depends on your target audience. If they would prefer shorter copy, use shorter copy. If they need longer, more informative copy, use longer copy. While the engines prefer longer text, always do what is best for your visitors first.

- **Do create META tags**. Remember to include META tags (written as described earlier) on each page.

- **Do have clean code**. Make sure your designer knows how to read code and hand code (if needed). Also make sure your designer validates your site's code before uploading it to the Internet.

- **Do use call files when needed**. As discussed, this can help free up the pathway the engine spiders will take when indexing your site.

- **Do create a site map**. A site map is similar to the table of contents in a book. It simply lists each page of your site with a very brief description of what can be found on those pages. This is very helpful to both your visitors and the search engines, as it allows each one to see and quickly click to each public page your site offers.

SEO Reporting

Many people believe you can optimize your site then walk away and have it perform at the same level forever. Just as you will need to keep up with the maintenance of your site design (as we discussed in earlier chapters), you'll also need to track and tweak your SEO campaign.

You want to be sure you're getting the results you're after. The only way to know is to track. What's involved with SEO reporting? First, you need to measure how the keyword search terms are performing. Most optimizers can provide you with a helpful monthly report that shows where each of your pages is ranking with the various engines. While the information is not 100% accurate (because the engines themselves change their terms of measurement so frequently), these reports do give a wonderful benchmark to go by. You can use the historical data from the reports to track your positioning from past to present. In addition, other metrics can also be tracked.

Unique Visitors: How many unique visitors are coming to your site? The number of unique visitors is a vital measurement. This tells you the number of new people who have visited your site. It does not include repeat visitors (yet another metric you can track), but rather it tells you how much new traffic your site is bringing in. You want this number to be high, so you can see your SEO campaign is working to attract and deliver new prospects to your site.

Repeat Visitors: Repeat visitors can also be measured and can tell you, as the name suggests, the number of people who have returned to your site for a second, third or even fourth visit.

Hits: While you still hear some people speak of the number of "hits" to their sites, this number is highly unstable and inaccurate. Never judge your site's success based on the number of hits. Basically speaking, one "hit" is calculated each time a file is opened. There are many files that come together to create a single web page. For instance, the page itself is one file. Each image or graphic can be another file. Java applets or Flash movies can have their own files. The design elements that make up page borders, etc., can have their own files. All in all, one single visit to your home page can actually trigger 10, 20, 30 or more "hits." Because virtually no two pages have the same number of elements, the measurement of "hits" is anything but accurate.

Where does this data come from? Most web site hosts offer basic data with regard to your site. However, if you want exceptional tracking of the exact pathways visitors take while on your site, the length of time they stay on each page, how often they return and to which pages and so on, you'll need to invest in a hardcore tracking service.

As more and more CPA sites come online and begin to compete for the keyphrases you have your sights on, your position may shift. Changes in search engine algos may cause shifts in your position. With the information the optimizer gleans from your site statistics (also called "stats") and from the ranking reports provided, s/he will recommend changes to your SEO campaign to make it more effective.

Is SEO worth it? Only you can decide the answer to that question. You should — at the very least — ask for quotes on SEO services, and then compare the cost of your current lead generation practices to the costs of an effective long-term SEO campaign. Quite often, SEO proves to be a highly valuable tool for CPA firms. The only way to know if SEO is right for you is to get the details and weigh the options based on your own needs, goals and budget.

What we've discussed in this chapter is referred to as "organic" or "natural" SEO. That's because, after you optimize the site, the pages (hopefully) show up in the engine's free results pages. Why hopefully? Because, as we mentioned previously, no one has all the information about what search engines are looking for. The algorithms are highly guarded secrets. No one — let me repeat — no one can guarantee organic search engine placement. If you are approached by a company that says they can guarantee you top 10 placements, hang up the phone. Many of these firms have been indicted on charges for fraud in the last year, and you would be wise to steer clear of them.

What do you need to know to interview and hire a search engine optimization firm? Use the worksheet on the following page to make sure you ask all the right questions.

Organic Search Engine Optimization Worksheet

Like CPA firms, all SEO companies are a little different. Each has its own set of services and policies it adheres to. Some may provide copywriting; some may not. Some may offer paid search and organic search; others may not. That's why it's important to ask.

1. What is your process for creating an SEO campaign? _____

_____

_____

_____

_____

2. Do you do your own keyword research? _____

3. If yes, what tools do you use for this research? _____

_____

_____

_____

4. Do you review the coding of my site to ensure it is clean and valid? _____

5. Do you use WYSIWYG editors when making changes to my code? _____

6. Do you write the META tags? _____

7. Do you offer link-building campaigns? _____

8. If so, please explain how you will obtain links to our site. _____

_____

_____

9. What type of tracking reports do you offer? _____

_____

_____

_____

10. What are your fees and how do you charge for your initial services?_____

_____

_____

_____

11. What do you offer in the way of maintenance and what are the charges for those services? _____

_____

_____

_____

12. Do you work month-to-month or do you require a contract? __

_____

_____

_____

If you need additional space, make copies of this worksheet or use notebook paper.

NOTE: Visit www.KLSWebSolutions.com/Worksheets to print worksheets from the Internet.

Pay-Per-Click:
Another Way To Be Found

"The value of e-commerce is not in the e, but in the commerce."
Octavio Paz
Mexican Writer

There is another way to get your site found on search engines. That practice is called Pay-Per-Click or PPC. PPC advertising has advantages. Unlike organic search engine optimization, you can control the budget for PPC; it's reliable, and your site can achieve high rankings immediately.

PPC Overview

Pay-per-click ads are those you find on Google or Yahoo! or other search engines that are usually designated with the title of "Sponsored Links" or some such title. When a visitor types in a keyphrase, ads that have paid to be shown alongside the organic results are populated on the page. These ads get their names because, each time a visitor clicks the link associated with one of those ads, the advertiser (you, in this case) is charged a fee. We spoke briefly about this in an earlier chapter. The revenue model is based on bidding for placement. The higher your bid per click, the higher your placement will be. Pay-Per-Click (PPC) is also sometimes called paid search or paid placement.

Because you're buying an advertisement rather than trying to be accepted into a free search engine datacenter (as with organic search), there is no need to alter your design, your coding or your copy to reflect any terms you might target in a PPC campaign.

To begin a PPC campaign, you will set up an account with each search engine. Once you do, you'll have a control panel where you can dictate your preferences for keywords and phrases, budget amounts, maximum spending per day/month, location and more.

Unlike organic search, PPC allows you to be featured in the search results immediately after your site is uploaded to the Internet. Organic search can take months to show results. This is a great way for CPAs with a brand new web presence to drive instant traffic to their sites.

Another excellent way to use your PPC campaign is in testing the headlines in your copy. Because you get immediate feedback from a PPC campaign about your keyword phrases, you can determine if the headlines you have selected are triggering the response you want. Simply use the headline for the copy of your PPC ad and see how high the click-through rates go. It's a quick and affordable way to do marketing research.

In addition, PPC is great for expanding your reach. Let's say you chose the keyphrase "CPA New York City" when you optimized your site for organic search. With PPC, you can easily also target the phrases "CPA New Jersey," "CPA Manhattan" or any other nearby town.

Google Adwords and Yahoo!/Overture are the two most well-known examples of PPC search engines today, although there are many more. Keep in mind, both Google and Yahoo!/Overture feed other search engines also. By placing ads with these two major PPC engines, you can also be featured on many other sites across the World Wide Web. Do the ads work? Do they get seen? Sure they do!

Visitor Response to Organic vs. PPC Results

Recently, research firms Enquiro and Did It released an eye-tracking study of how visitors reacted to Google search results pages. They found that the attraction to organic search results (left side of the page) in the top, left corner especially, was extremely strong. One hundred percent of the site visitors looked at the organic search results in positions one, two and three. Position four was viewed by 85% of the visitors and positions five through 10 (on the first page of results) were viewed by between 60% and 20% of the visitors respectively. Additionally, organic results (as a whole) were viewed by 80%-100% of the visitors while paid results were viewed by between 10%-50% of the visitors. What does it all mean?

Visitors to Google always look at the top three results in the upper left-hand corner of the organic search results. They frequently look at the paid search results (PPC) on the right-hand side of the page. If you're going to do SEO, you need to do it aggressively and aim for the top three positions in organic results.

Does that mean you should discount PPC advertising? Not at all. As you've already seen, PPC has great advantages and is seen by a lot of visitors. In fact, many companies only do PPC because of the full control they have over their campaigns. You'll have to weigh the options and costs and decide which is best for you. Many businesses think PPC is tops! For this reason, PPC advertising has grown rapidly.

A July 2004 report by Jupiter Research estimated that online advertising would increase to $16.1 billion by 2009. The reason for the rapid growth? It's that businesses have found something that works well for them. They can attract people (at a low cost) who are looking for their goods or services. What's better than that!

For the latest information on this topic, make sure to visit **payperclickanalyst.com**. This site provides a lot of very helpful and up-to-date information on this topic.

Getting Started

If you decide to use PPC, you will need to research your keywords, determine what locations (local, regional, national, international) can see your web site, how much to bid on each keyword phrase and set your budget.

Research

As we mentioned in the previous chapter, a key element for both organic and PPC campaigns is researching your keyword phrases. If you have already done this for your organic search, there is really no need to recreate the wheel. You should start with that list and then expand it. PPC engines normally offer their own keyword research tools. While I wouldn't use this research for organic optimization (because of the limited data provided), it is very valid for PPC campaigns.

Once you have chosen the keyphrases you want to be found for, you'll want to check the per-click price for each. Terms related to CPAs should be very reasonable. However, terms related to marketing or web hosting or automobiles can cost $10 or even $20 per click — and are changing daily! Cost plays a major role in deciding which keyphrases most people will include in their campaigns.

Location Specific

As you set up your PPC campaign criteria, one option is setting your location. For example, a CPA firm with one office in Dallas, Texas, is not interested in a prospective client in Idaho. This firm can and should limit their location to Dallas, Texas, and nearby towns. Therefore, someone using the search term "CPA Chesterfield, Idaho" will not see a PPC campaign that is restricted to only show up for searchers in certain parts of Texas.

This feature not only works for states, but also cities. You can include and exclude in either a broad or narrow fashion depending on your specific needs. If you have offices in Dallas, Texas; Naples, Florida and Williamsburg, Virginia, you can include all the neighboring towns for each of the offices if you want.

This is a very powerful feature in PPC advertising, as it allows you to be highly accurate in finding clients for your business. You don't want to pay for leads that are a dead end right from the start.

Bidding

When someone clicks on your link and visits your site, you are charged whatever amount you placed a bid for. In a simple example, if someone in your industry is paying $2.00 per click for a keyword phrase and is ranking in the top sponsored ad position, you could bid $2.01 to overtake them and rank #1 in sponsored results.

However, I would not advise fighting for the #1 position. A Cornell University study found that many prospects blindly click on the highest listing just because it's in the top spot. This can cause unnecessary and costly clicks to your site that don't deliver the needed return on investment (ROI). Therefore, a better position may be in the second or third spaces.

You also have the option of setting limits on the amount you spend per day and other monetary limits. These also affect where your listing shows in the results. For instance, if your competitor is only willing to spend $30 a day, his exposure is likely to run out before that of someone who spends $50 or $60 a day. After his $30 for the day runs out, you might be moved to the #1 slot by default because the competitor's ad no longer shows.

Cyclical keyword phrases are another thing to keep in mind. During certain points of the year, you may want to turn off certain keyword phrases, so they don't show in the results at all. For example, the keyword phrase "Dallas, Texas tax returns" may not be a good phrase to have during April unless you have time for extra clients.

Bidding on keywords is both an art and a science. You don't want to overspend on keyword bids, but you also don't want to end up at the bottom of the results. Remember that Enquiro and Did It released an eye-tracking study? It also showed the eye movements of visitors when they looked at PPC ads in the two spots. The highest positioned sponsored ads are across the top of the Google results page. Others are down the right side. After the third ad on the right side, visuals dropped dramatically to only 20%. The upper middle looks like prime property. Not too high so your ads get abused by those with trigger-happy fingers, but not so low you don't get noticed.

We once had a prospective client approach us that was dissatisfied with the PPC campaign he had set up for himself. His first comment was, "I'm not getting any business from my campaign!" When we took a look at the campaign, he had bid the minimum for all his keyword phrases, and his ranking was near the bottom of the search results. Because of that, he had created a very affordable campaign that was delivering virtually no clients. Balance, balance, balance.

Your Budget

In their book, *Search Engine Marketing, Inc.*, Mike Moran and Bill Hunt discuss the challenges in creating a budget for your paid search campaigns. To summarize their thoughts on this — Yahoo! /Overture is fairly straightforward. You look at what others are bidding, assume that you can get a high spot, examine keyword demand and estimate your click-through rate. When you do that, you can come up with a reasonable estimate of costs. In Google, you are not given information on how much the top spots cost or the click-through rate. You are at the mercy of Google's estimate, which can be off by more than 25%. The best advice for Google users: create your campaign, monitor it very closely during the first month and adjust accordingly.

Monitoring

As we discussed in previous chapters, one wonderful thing about web sites is their ability to give you concrete, immediate feedback on the money you spend. In your PPC campaign, everything is measurable and — at least for the first few months — you should monitor everything.

Google gives you the ability to track keyphrases separated into various campaigns. You can organize this as you see fit. You can then view the number of impressions, the number of clicks, the cost per click, the cap for per-day spending, the click-through rate, locations and much more.

You will need to periodically review your bidding strategy, keyword selection and ad description as well as the information available in your account. If you review, or have a professional review, and adjust accordingly, you can refine your PPC campaign to the point that you gain almost perfect clients that are searching for your exact services — and you can do so automatically, 24 hours a day, for a very reasonable price.

Most companies hire someone to manage their PPC campaign at least for the first few months. After that point, when you become familiar with the settings and features of Google and/or Yahoo!/Overture, you may choose to take over the management of the campaign. I recommend at least starting with professional help. Use the worksheet on the following page to guide you in collecting information for your own use or to share with the PPC company of choice. Keep in mind, many SEO companies also offer PPC, so you may be able to use one firm for both functions.

Pay-Per-Click Advertising Worksheet

1. What keyphrases did you choose for use in your organic SEO campaign? (Use these as your starting point or share them with your PPC manager.)

_____

_____

_____

_____

_____

_____

2. Do these also show good results in PPC research? _____

_____

_____

3. Will you need to narrow results only for specific locations? _____

_____

4. If yes, which locations? _____

_____

_____

_____

5. If the information is available, what are the current top three bids for each of the keyphrases you want to target?

Keyphrase: _____   Keyphrase: _____

Bid 1 – $ _____   Bid 1 – $ _____

Bid 2 – $ _____   Bid 2 – $ _____

Bid 3 – $ _____   Bid 3 – $ _____

Keyphrase: _____   Keyphrase: _____

Bid 1 – $ _____   Bid 1 – $ _____

Bid 2 – $ _____   Bid 2 – $ _____

Bid 3 – $ _____   Bid 3 – $ _____

Keyphrase: _____   Keyphrase: _____

Bid 1 – $ _____   Bid 1 – $ _____

Bid 2 – $ _____   Bid 2 – $ _____

Bid 3 – $ _____   Bid 3 – $ _____

Keyphrase: _____   Keyphrase: _____

Bid 1 – $ _____   Bid 1 – $ _____

Bid 2 – $ _____   Bid 2 – $ _____

Bid 3 – $ _____   Bid 3 – $ _____

6. Where do you want to be listed in the results? (#1, #2, #3, etc.)

_____

7. What budget do you have for your PPC campaign? _____

_____

8. How much does that allow you to spend per day? _____

9. Will you set up and monitor your own campaign? _____

_____

If not, you'll want to give this worksheet, along with your budget figures, to the SEO company who will handle PPC for you.

If you need additional space, make copies of this worksheet or use notebook paper.

NOTE: Visit www.KLSWebSolutions.com/Worksheets to print worksheets from the Internet.

11

Other Avenues for Promotion: Local Search, Directories and Specialty Listings

"Think globally, search locally . . ."
Paul Levine
GM of Yahoo! Local

Search engines (either organic or PPC) are the primary vehicles for people looking for information on the Internet. However, there are also other mediums people use to search for information. Local search, directories and specialty engines are other alternatives to organic and PPC, and are worth including in your site promotion strategy.

While directory submissions can be costly and time-consuming, if you choose to hire a SEO firm, they can create and perform all directory submissions for you.

Local Listings

The major search engines have become aware of the value of local search, which is searching in your local area only as opposed to searching the entire World Wide Web for products or services. For

CPA firms this presents additional opportunities for client development. There are three local search engines currently on the scene: Yahoo!, Google and Verizon SuperPages.

Yahoo!: This service is offered directly off the Yahoo! home page. If a searcher clicks on the Local Search button, they are prompted for their search term and address or zip code. Results are listed first for pay-per-click web sites and then local organic results are shown that include address, phone number, map link and distance to the business.

Companies can sign up for Yahoo!'s Basic Listing (free) or pay for an Enhanced Listing. The Basic Listing includes business name, address, phone, link to web site, operating information, services provided and five categories (search terms) that a business might be found under. The Enhanced Listing costs a nominal monthly fee and enables you to also include company tagline, business description, two links to promotional offers, up to ten photos and performance reports.

Google Local: Also offered on the home page as a separate search product. Searchers input a search term and a zip code, or the name of a town or city.

The Google service offers powerful, user-friendly mapping technology and local business information — including business locations, contact information and driving directions. The search results include integrated local search results where the searcher can find business location and contact information all in one place integrated on the map. For example, if the site visitor searches for "CPA in San Jose," locations of relevant listings and phone numbers appear on the map. A searcher can also view additional information, like hours of operation, types of payment accepted and reviews.

To populate the search results, Google collects business information from numerous web sites, Yellow Pages directories and other sources.

SuperPages.com: SuperPages provides Yellow Book information on their site and also feeds this information to MSN.com,

Infospace.com and Lycos.com. Verizon SuperPages is now allowing businesses to add or update their listings with searchable keywords, web site link, a business graphic and custom text.

Directory Listings

Directories are listings of web sites by subject (rather than keywords) that are maintained by human editors. Because of the human intervention, submitting to directories is much more time intensive than getting listed with organic search engines where a spider comes and crawls your site. You must provide a lot of information to the directory editor regarding your site, find the best category for your business and wait for your site to be indexed, which takes a longer period of time than spidering.

Directory listings will include a site title and site description. While you are requested to make a suggestion of which category you feel your site should fall under, you are not guaranteed placement in that category. The final decision is solely up to the editor. Directory listings (like most things in life) have pros and cons.

Pros

- Search engines like directory listings because they give an authoritative link back to your site.
- Directories give you one more way to gain exposure for your site.
- Visitors coming from a directory link will be highly targeted.
- The cost is relatively inexpensive.

Cons

- The majority of web surfers use search engines to find what they are looking for as opposed to directories.

- There may be a cost for inclusion, usually around $300-$400 (one-time fee).
- There is no guarantee your site will be accepted, and, if it is rejected, you forfeit your payment.

Right now there are two well-known directories: Yahoo! and the Open Directory Project (also known as DMOZ).

Yahoo!: The grandmother of the Internet. In 1994, to help people find information on the Internet, a small company in California, oddly named Yahoo!, began categorizing web sites by category. There was no search capability for visitors in the beginning. This directory allowed searchers to drill down through categories until they found the appropriate topic. Sites that fell into the particular category were listed in alphabetical order. Searchers had to manually scan each listing to see which site they wanted to visit. Narrowing a search was difficult, at best, and the results were lacking in accuracy. Still, back in the day, Yahoo! was a search pioneer and the hottest ticket in town. At that time, it was free to submit your site, and chances were very good that you would be accepted. Times have changed!

Today, Yahoo! is better known for its search engine than its directory. You must pay several hundred dollars to submit to the Yahoo! Directory, and this does not guarantee you will be accepted.

Open Directory Project: The Open Directory Project was founded under a different name, GnuHoo, in 1998. It is currently the only major directory that is 100% free of charge. It is constructed and maintained by a vast, global community of volunteer editors. For this reason, gaining inclusion may take a long period of time.

Also called DMOZ, the Open Directory Project is operated by Netscape. DMOZ stands for "Directory Mozilla" because of its loose association with Netscape's Mozilla product.

Specialty Directories

Directories that cover a single subject area are called specialty, niche or vertical directories. Links from these directories can be very beneficial to your business, as they tend to attract pre-qualified prospects. Specialty directories may include those for CPAs in general along with a variety of niche practices. When someone finds your firm via one of these directories, s/he has already done a good deal of research. This prospect already knows what s/he wants and has clicked through to your site to see if you offer it. If they find that you do have what they are looking for, they will contact you. Because they've been through this self-imposed process, they are likely to be easy to convert to a paying client. Search engines also like these directories because they provide an authoritative link to your site.

One site that is currently popular (and is worth spending the money on) is AccountantsWorld.com. This directory is using PPC advertising to bring qualified leads to its site. It also has high organic search engine listings.

This is good news for you. Because AccountantsWorld.com is paying big bucks for PPC and organic search listings, you can benefit from their success. Just list your site on their site to increase your traffic. The bad news for you if you are listed at AccountantsWorld.com is that you are in direct competition with other accountants in your area. The pros outweigh the cons for this site, in my opinion. My recommendation is to list with AccountantsWorld.com, as it is a wonderful place to drum up qualified leads.

12

Ezines: Convert, Retain and Sell

"You are what you repeatedly do.
Excellence is not an event — it is a habit."
Aristotle
Greek Philosopher

Ezines have become a crucial form of communication with clients, prospective clients, vendors and colleagues. Since ezines are very cost-effective and time-efficient tools, it's not surprising that their popularity has grown so quickly. Besides quick communication, ezines can be exceptional lead generation tools, selling tools and client maintenance tools.

I started an email postcard several years ago when I founded a web design business targeting small businesses in Westchester County, New York. I was meeting so many people at networking events that I had no hope of keeping in touch with them on a regular basis through phone calls. As a result, I started a monthly ezine that gave people links to various web sites I thought they would find useful. Since my ezine is very short, I call it *PostCards from the Web*. One of the interesting things about this is that when I meet someone again at a networking event who reads my *PostCards*, they act like they know me very well even though we only met briefly many months or years before. My ezine gives them a more personal relationship with my company and me.

In addition, my *PostCards* ezine allows me to keep in touch with my current clients and gain work from them on a regular basis. Since they see me in their inboxes once a month, they are constantly reminded to use my company when they have web design needs.

How do you create an ezine for your firm? There are many ways to go about it, and the types of ezines are as diverse as individual people. There are some things, however, that are necessities — the first of which is to have a custom ezine design.

Ezine Templates

Ezine templates are often provided by various CPA-focused web sites. The idea is good, but the results are less than stellar. The idea of ezine templates is to make it easy for CPAs to publish an ezine. However, the same articles are often used in multiple ezines meaning your publication may contain the exact same information as competing firms. In addition, the same design templates are frequently used by numerous firms. How embarrassing would it be to email prospective clients the same exact ezine as another CPA firm? To ensure quality and be on the safe side, it's always best to hire a designer to custom-create your ezine design.

List Hosting

In order to produce an ezine that doesn't take over all your free time, it truly should be automated. That will mean finding and using a list host. List hosts are web-based companies who manage your ezine. They don't create it, but they manage the subscriber and mailing functions, so you don't have to. For instance, when a visitor comes to your site, s/he may choose to subscribe to your ezine. If you have a list host, your visitor will fill out your subscriber form. Instantly, they will receive a confirmation of their subscription and a welcome message from your firm. Should they ever choose to unsubscribe, this action is handled by the list host as well. You can just imagine, once your ezine gets up to a few hundred or a few thousand (highly possible) subscribers, what an enormous time waster it would be to manually subscribe, welcome and unsubscribe all these people.

In addition, list hosts handle the cleaning of your subscriber base of bounced email addresses (those that were rejected because they were no longer valid, etc.), the actual mass mailing of your ezine, personalization, open-rate tracking, click-through tracking and more. Let's look at each feature, so you can see why they are important.

Mailing Service: The larger your subscriber base gets, the more you will appreciate having a list host to mail your ezine for you. In addition to taking up a good deal of bandwidth (depending on the format you choose), sending mass mailings from your current email address may be against your hosting service's terms of service due to spam regulations. Also, many web hosts put a limit of how many emails your account may receive or send during a certain period of time. Because list hosts use their own web server, this saves you from violating any terms of service or email regulations that might get you in trouble with your web hosting company.

Personalization: Using the recipient's name in the subject line and message of your ezine is known to increase open rates by 27%. This same form of personalization within the ezine improved click-through rates by 6.89% on average, according to a September 2005 study by Mailer-Mailer email statistics report. That's primarily because people like to feel as though they are known. They like to be addressed and recognized. Most list hosts offer personalization of the subject line and body text as a built-in feature.

Open-Rate Tracking: This metric is exactly what it sounds like. It tells you the number of people who opened your ezine. This feature only works, however, with HTML (graphic) ezines. A tiny, unnoticeable pixel (dot) is placed at the top of your ezine before it is mailed out for tracking purposes. Each time someone opens your ezine in their inbox; the pixel adds them to the final count. This feature is not always offered by every list host. I recommend that you go with a list host that provides open-rate tracking. This is the only way you'll know if your ezine is paying off. If people aren't reading your newsletter, you'll need to make adjustments to increase interest. But how will you know if they are or are not reading it unless you can see the open-rate statistics?

Click-Through Tracking: Similar to open-rate tracking, click-through tracking uses specially designed links to account for how many times subscribers visit each link in your ezine. Click-through tracking works for both HTML and plain text ezines. For instance, if, in your ezine, you made reference to some information on your site and gave a link to a page where the information could be found, you could see how many readers clicked through to the page using this metric. Not all list hosts offer this feature, so you'll want to look and be sure yours does.

Three of the best-known list hosts are:

www.ConstantContact.com

www.AWeber.com

www.Lyris.com

Getting Subscribers

So, you've got a list host. Now, you just need some subscribers for your list host to manage! How do you get them? Most list hosts give you (or your web designer) the ability to create subscription forms to include on your site. You'll want to put this form on your home page (bare minimum) and every other public page of your site, so visitors can sign up to receive your ezines.

Once they subscribe, the list host will send an immediate, automated confirmation to the subscriber asking her/him to verify that s/he was really the person who requested a subscription. This is referred to as "double opt-in." It is a standard practice that helps prevent people from spamming your subscription form.

After the subscriber verifies his/her intent, a welcome message (that you (or your copywriter) have written and uploaded to the list host) is automatically sent to the subscriber. That's it! You now have subscribers!

You'll want to include unsubscribe instructions at the bottom of every issue of your ezine, just in case someone chooses to no longer receive your publication.

HTML vs. Plain Text

As you saw in a previous chapter, there are two forms of ezine formats: HTML and plain text. I'll paste an example of each on the next two pages, so you won't have to turn back in the book to view them.

Each has its own set of advantages and disadvantages. Let's take a look at both, so you can decide which is better for you.

HTML: There's no doubt: HTML looks good! There are as many different HTML designs as there are web sites. In fact, with HTML, your ezine design can match your web design. You can include pictures, tables, graphs, charts and any other images you want. If it could be placed on your web site, you can include it in your HTML ezine. Open-rate tracking is available with HTML also. On the downside, HTML takes up more "space" than plain text. Because it's a larger file, people with slow dial-up Internet connections may get frustrated waiting on it to open in their email box. Many years ago, some web hosts had trouble displaying HTML messages in email boxes, but that is no longer the case. Practically anyone with any type of email address should be able to view HTML.

Plain Text: Plain text — if formatted nicely — can be an acceptable alternative. However, plain text ezines will never look as professional as HTML. Plain text does take up less space and loads instantly in email boxes regardless of whether the reader is using dial-up or high speed. Some people, because of personal taste, prefer plain text. Almost every list host will include the option of sending a plain text version when you send an HTML ezine, so it makes sense to take advantage of that and please everybody.

January 2006

Kaja's Design Tips
The Home Designer's Resource

Dear Kaja,
Welcome to the **Kaja Gam Design E-Zine.** Here you'll find tips and ideas to help you tackle your home improvement projects.

The Kitchen of Today

by Kaja Gam

Is this the year to remodel your kitchen? According to House & Garden magazine's January 2006 special report, the kitchen has doubled in size since the 1970s. That means it finally gets the recognition it deserves as the most important room in the house. Kitchens designed today will last for a very long time because of their new innovations including efficient space layout, hi-tech appliances, cabinet components and durable materials. All this makes for a functional, convenient and beautiful living space. From floor to ceiling, here's what you need to know about the kitchen of your dreams.

The kitchen is integral to our lives. Everyone in the home makes use of this room. The name "kitchen" and the image of the housewife donning an apron and toiling away behind closed doors are history. Many attempts at naming this new multi-functional room have been made: great room, family all-room and eat-live kitchen just begin to describe the function of this central hub of our lives.

What they all sum up is the same reality: the kitchen is the axis of our lives. Entertaining friends, spending time with family, talking about the day's events and cooking up a little romance are all done in the kitchen. Read More...

View kitchens designed by Kaja.

Next Month's Topic

Create Your Own Mudroom
If your house doesn't have a mudroom, it should. And it can! Find out how to transform current space into this necessary space.

January 2006
Kaja's Design Tips
The Home Designer's Resource

Dear Kaja,

Welcome to the Kaja
Gam Design E-Zine. Here you'll find tips and
ideas to help you tackle
your home improvement projects.

~~~~~~

The Kitchen of Today
by Kaja Gam

Is this the year to remodel your kitchen? According
to House & Garden magazine's January 2006 special
report, the kitchen has doubled in size since the
1970s. That means it finally gets the recognition it
deserves as the most important room in the house.
Kitchens designed today will last for a very long time
because of their new innovations including efficient
space layout, hi-tech appliances, cabinet
components and durable materials. All this makes for
a functional, convenient and beautiful living space.
From floor to ceiling, here's what you need to know
about the kitchen of your dreams.

The kitchen is integral to our lives. Everyone in the
home makes use of this room. The name "kitchen"
and the image of the housewife donning an apron
and toiling away behind closed doors are history.
Many attempts at naming this new multi-functional
room have been made: great room, family all-room
and eat-live kitchen just begin to describe the
function of this central hub of our lives.

What they all sum up is the same reality: the
kitchen is the axis of our lives. Entertaining friends,
spending time with family, talking about the day's
events and cooking up a little romance are all done in
the kitchen.

Scheduling

Ezines may be published daily, biweekly, weekly, semiweekly, monthly or quarterly. Technically, you can publish at any interval you choose, but these are the most common time frames. Whichever schedule you decide to follow, make sure you are consistent. Subscribers will get frustrated and lose interest if you publish using an erratic schedule.

Sections

A Radicati Group study conducted in April 2005 reported that most business employees receive 133 email messages per day. That number is climbing with 160 emails per day expected by 2009. Much of this email is spam (unsolicited email), sales notices or other promotional-type messages. You, yourself, know how annoying it is to get "another" sales message in your inbox. For that reason, your ezine material has to be relevant and timely. What type of information would that be?

An ezine sent out in early November that discusses last-minute tax-saving strategies would be welcome by many of your current clients and prospects. The ezine could highlight four or five tax-saving ideas and end with a paragraph that encourages the subscriber to call or email you if they have any further questions or concerns. The approach is subtle, but incredibly successful. What else could you include?

Welcome: A greeting welcoming the reader to a new issue and letting them know what to expect. A letter to the editor type thing. If you have any special news, you might share it here.

Feature Article: Some ezines include one feature article on a relevant subject; some include two. Some, however, don't include any. Rather they give snippets of several articles from relevant online sources with links to where the reader can view the entire text. Each has pros and cons. Creating your own material can take time. Yet, so can researching, locating and gaining reprint permission for other people's articles. Then there is the question of what your subscriber base would rather have. Would they prefer articles written by your firm (to show your areas of expertise)? Would they find it annoying to have to click to the web to read the articles?

Some do, and others don't mind at all. Yet another option is to do a Question & Answer ezine with no articles at all. You would simply answer questions you've been asked by your clients or prospects and send those in your mailing.

Resources: This section is usually pretty popular because it (in its premier form) gives valuable resources readers can save and use repeatedly. A basic example would be exact links to direct pages of your state's Department of Revenue site where visitors could find specific forms, answers to questions, etc.

Question & Answer: If you choose to include an article, you can also include a question and answer section as well.

Tax Updates: Have there been updates your readers should know about? New deductions they need to save receipts for? Past deductions that are no longer available? Increases in IRA contributions? Include an overview in your ezine, and then direct readers back to your site for the details.

Deadlines: Procrastination is one of our favorite pastimes as human beings. Everyone appreciates a gentle nudge as a reminder of an upcoming deadline. (Especially if missing that deadline involves incurring a penalty!)

Company News: Anything exciting happening in your firm? Tell your readers. You don't want to get too involved with this section, but including little tidbits about new employees (and how they can be helpful to clients), expansions, office moves, etc. is a great way to make your ezine more personal.

Informative ezines build loyalty, trust and interest. Through your ezine you become a trusted provider of valuable information and gain the status of a trusted advisor to your clients.

Subject Line

An interesting subject line is absolutely vital in any type of email marketing. Just as much emphasis should be placed on the subject line of your ezine as is placed on the headlines in your copy. Just like the magazines at the local grocery store snatch your attention in their direction (whether we'd like to admit it or not!), your email is competing with all the other emails that have come through and want to be read. The subject line is all the reader has to go by when deciding if s/he actually opens and reads the message or deletes it.

Your subject line must be brief (you have only about 35 readable characters (including spaces)) and should attract attention and make an impact. If your subject line does not attract attention, your ezine runs the risk of never being opened and being banished to the recycle bin.

So what exactly makes for a good subject line? Here are three ideas.

1) State Your Article Title.

Do you have a catchy article title that would also make a great subject line? Use it! For example:

Small Businesses in Danger of Major Tax Hikes

New Tax Deductions on the Way

2) Evoke Curiosity.

We're all nosey to a point. Our curiosity gets the best of us, and we want to know more. That's not only true when it comes to watching movie previews on TV. It's also true for email as well. Some of the best subject lines hook readers by piquing their curiosity, and then reel them in to read the entire message.

Can These New Deductions Save You Big?

Got a Hybrid Car? Get a Tax Deduction!

3) Make an Offer.

Whether a product, a service or a proposal, you want to tell people up front about your best deals, your fastest delivery or your grandest idea. Get their attention right off the bat, and you'll likely have your message read. (It's even better if your offer happens to be time sensitive.) Examples include:

Free Past Tax Return Reviews Thru Oct.

Free College Planning Seminar 7/15

If you catch your readers right up front with interesting subject lines, they'll reward you with their attention.

Ezine Articles

Once readers open your ezine, you'll have to keep them interested by providing exceptional material. How do you find a consistent source of ideas to write about?

One of the best methods for finding content for your newsletter is to sign up for ezines from other companies to get a sense of what others are writing about. Keep a folder of future ezine ideas, including newspaper and magazine articles, inspirations that hit you in the middle of the night, articles you read on web sites, articles you read in other ezines, etc. Look at this folder before you decide on your topic.

Other ideas are provided courtesy of Janet Attard. She offers these five ideas for writing articles and getting your newsletter published:

1) Hire a freelancer writer

Sure, it's your company newsletter, but there's no reason any of it has to be written by you or your staff. A good freelance writer who knows your industry can get the job done quickly and professionally. Depending on your preferences and the deal you cut with the writer, the articles can carry the writer's byline or go out under your name or the company's name without attribution to the writer.

2) Invite guest experts to write for you.

You've probably met a variety of people in your industry who are experts in their field — but don't directly compete with you. Tap into their knowledge — and stroke their egos — by asking them to write a guest column for you occasionally. In lieu of payment, offer them a link to their web site and short author's bio at the end of the article.

3) Ask your readers to contribute articles.

Readers love to share their experiences, and having them do so builds up a feeling of community for your newsletter and site. Include a note in one or more newsletters telling them you'd love to hear how they use your products or information, and let them know you may publish some of the best submissions. (Don't promise to publish everything. Not everything you get will be worth publishing.) When you use a submission, be sure to archive a copy of the newsletter on your website. Then send the reader an email with a link to the archived article. That way the contributor can forward the link to all their friends. If you've included a newsletter sign-up box on the page, those friends may join your mailing list, too.

4) Check out article distribution sites

Article distribution sites (free web content and free ezine article sites) are sites that aggregate articles from many different writers who want to have their articles distributed and made available for reprint. The writers upload the articles to the sites, and give blanket permission to reprint their articles as long as their author's resource box and contact information is retained. The writers benefit by getting their names and website links published on sites that use their articles. You benefit by getting free editorial content. Not all the editorial material is of equal quality, but if you pick through the article listings, you may find articles by authors, experts and public speakers that will be perfect for your newsletter. You can find article distribution sites by searching the web for "Free Web Content," "Free Articles" or "Ezine Articles." You'll also find a list of sites on the resource link below.

5) Hire a freelance editor or virtual assistant to produce the newsletter.

Articles aren't the only things you can outsource. You can outsource the production, too. A freelance editor or virtual assistant can stay in contact with your authors and writers to be sure that copy gets in on time, is edited, spell-checked and set up in your newsletter template.

Monitoring

The wonderful thing about most ezine software is you can monitor who is clicking on what stories. After sending your ezine, you can see who opened your email, which links generated the most interest and who clicked on each link. If your ezine is sent out with multiple stories, you can find out who clicked on the story to read more. You can use the information from your campaign to understand the needs and wants of your readers, so you can adjust your focus as needed.

It is also important to look at this information over time. Is your subscription list increasing every month? Are your open rates remaining high? Was there one topic that people were really interested in? Getting and using the feedback from your ezine campaigns is very important for continued success.

Use the worksheet on the next page to be sure you've covered all the steps to creating a great ezine.

Ezine Creation Worksheet

List Host: _____

URL: _____

Cost per month: $_____

For how many subscribers? _____

Does this list host offer:

❑ Double opt-in subscription   ❑ Bounce handling

❑ Automated mailing   ❑ Future mailing

❑ Personalization   ❑ Open-rate tracking

❑ Click-rate tracking   ❑ HTML and plain text

List Host: _____

URL: _____

Cost per month: $_____

For how many subscribers? _____

Does this list host offer:

❑ Double opt-in subscription   ❑ Bounce handling

❑ Automated mailing   ❑ Future mailing

❑ Personalization   ❑ Open-rate tracking

❑ Click-rate tracking   ❑ HTML and plain text

List Host: _____

URL: _____

Cost per month: $_____

For how many subscribers? _____

Does this list host offer:

❑ Double opt-in subscription   ❑ Bounce handling

❑ Automated mailing   ❑ Future mailing

❑ Personalization   ❑ Open-rate tracking

❑ Click-rate tracking   ❑ HTML and plain text

List Host: _____

URL: _____

Cost per month: $_____

For how many subscribers? _____

Does this list host offer:

❑ Double opt-in subscription   ❑ Bounce handling

❑ Automated mailing   ❑ Future mailing

❑ Personalization   ❑ Open-rate tracking

❑ Click-rate tracking   ❑ HTML and plain text

My publishing schedule will be:

❑ daily   ❑ weekly   ❑ semimonthly

❑ monthly   ❑ bimonthly   ❑ quarterly

other: _____

With regard to articles, I will include:

❑ one custom article per issue

❑ two custom articles per issue

❑ articles written by others and used by permission

❑ snippets of articles with links to the entire text online

If you need additional space, make copies of this worksheet or use notebook paper.

NOTE: Visit www.KLSWebSolutions.com/Worksheets to print work-sheets from the Internet.

13

Maintaining Your Site and Tracking Your Results

"Success is a journey, not a destination."
Ben Sweetland
Author

It is interesting how we are suddenly struck by a thought or concept that we should have been aware of all along. Somewhere in the back of our minds, a little voice begins to speak or a sudden inspiration hits us. It gels a lot of the things that we have been doing, and we have a eureka moment. I just had this recently with regard to my clients and their web sites.

The clients that are benefiting the most from their web sites are the ones that have incorporated them into their businesses. It is not a special project that gets a lot of focus for a period of time and then shelved away. Their web site has become part of their marketing and sales strategy. They are focused on their web site as a part of their everyday business routine. To enhance your accounting firm through your web site, you need to think about it and its progress at least weekly if not daily. You need a paradigm shift in your thinking: your web site is not a special project; your web site is an iterative process. With this process is where web site maintenance begins.

Keep It Current

Let's start with the basics. The first thing that you must do after your web site is launched is make plans to keep it current. We've all been there — surfing around the Internet when we happen upon a site. It looks like it has the information or services we want. As we browse, we begin to notice that this site has stale information. Maybe it's the current events section bearing a date of 2002 or an article touting out-of-date information that tips you off. Suddenly you realize this site hasn't been updated in a long time. Do you suddenly lose interest and return to your original search? If you're like me, you do!

Your web site needs to be in the forefront of your mind. When you add a key employee, your site should be updated. When you move, change the contact information on your site. Received information about new tax laws, put them on your site. Any time your firm has a life-changing event or any time you receive information your client base should know about, you must update your web site.

How embarrassing will it be the next time a prospect you've met at a networking event asks for your web site address? You'll look down at the floor and say, "We have a web site, but it's sorely out of date. Can I just mail you the information?" Imagine giving out your business card and having to cross out your company's URL (web address) because you'd rather not have prospects or clients visit something that's out of date. You would be mortified! Before you even make the decision to develop your site, you need to commit to handling (or hiring someone to handle) the necessary maintenance on the back end.

Lead Enhancing Maintenance

It is vital to update the contact information on your site. How can prospects and clients locate you if your phone number, physical address, PO box or email address is outdated? To really have an impressive site, however, you should update the information at least once a month for visitors.

Links to other sites must be maintained. Because the web moves and changes at the speed of light, sites appear and disappear before your very eyes. Once per month you should have someone check all the external links (links that lead to other sites) on your site to ensure they are still "live." It's frustrating for visitors to find "dead" links, and it makes you look unprofessional. There are many software packages that will check the outgoing links from your site and notify you if there are dead links, so you, or your designer, can change or remove them.

If you include "What's New" or "Current News" pages, they must absolutely be kept up to date. How silly would it be to have a current events page with outdated information?

If you arrange a monthly maintenance program with your designer, you can rest easy knowing s/he will keep you looking professional. If you plan to maintain your site in-house, be sure to create a checklist, so you don't miss updating any sections.

Web Statistics

Web statistics (stats) are the report card for your web site. You find them most commonly as a portion of your web hosting account. You can also purchase more detailed software packages or online services that offer a tremendous amount of information, but the basic stats that come from your web host are a good start. This information can be very useful and powerful when interpreted properly. It basically lets you know how many people have come to your site, how long they stayed, which pages they visited, what hours or days had the most activity, where visitors came from and more.

Why would you care? Having a website and not looking at the statistics is like running a company without ever reconciling the bank statements. You need to look at the details of your site's operations to make important, strategic decisions.

So what information can your web site stats provide? Here are some great examples: feedback on how well your navigation is performing, how long visitors stay at your site, what search terms people used to find your site and more. Your web stats are a goldmine of information! But just what, exactly, does this information mean?

Detailed Statistics

Let's look at the most common stats in detail to get a better idea of how site stats can be of help.

Number of Hits: Back in the old days, sites would brag about having millions of "hits" to their web site every day. As we quickly found out, a hit is nothing to brag about! As explained in the SEO chapter of this book, basically speaking, one "hit" is calculated each time a file is opened. There are many files that come together to create a single web page. For instance, the page itself is one file. Each image or graphic can be another file. Java applets or Flash movies can have their own files. The design elements that make up page borders, etc. can have their own files. All in all, one single visit to your home page can actually trigger 10, 20, 30 or more "hits." Because virtually no two pages have the same number of elements, the measurement of "hits" is anything but accurate.

This is a very misleading and worthless measurement as far as I'm concerned. I only bring it up as some still brag about the number of hits to their web sites. I want you to be aware of how useless this number is.

Number of Visitors: This is the total number of visitors that come to your site over a given period of time. This number includes people that may have come once or may have returned several times.

Number of Unique Visitors: Unique visitors are only counted once regardless of how many times they visit. This is the best unit of measure for tracking email campaigns, newsletters, etc. because you get a fresh count each time.

Length of Visit: As you might imagine, this tells how much time your visitors are, on average, spending on your site. The time users spend on your site is a great indication of how useful and compelling they find your content. By keeping your site's materials updated and adding new information frequently, you can effectively increase the time people are spending on your site.

Depth of Visit: This metric shows how deep into your site your visitors have gone. For example, you can see how many visitors only viewed one page and left, how many viewed ten web pages and so on. This can be a good indicator of whether your navigation is effective and your content is compelling.

Top Keywords: This report shows the actual keywords or phrases visitors typed into search engines to find your site. The art of search engine placement requires keyword reporting in order to know which words and phrases are successfully leading people to your site and from which search engines. With this knowledge, you will know which search engines you need to step up your strategy for and which ones you are having success with. Obviously, this information is very important if you are working on search engine optimization, but it is also important to review if you aren't.

Top Search Engines: This report shows referral traffic from the search engines visitors used to find your site. With this report, you can tell at a glance which search engines are sending you the most traffic.

Top Referrers: A "referrer" is a web site page that contains a link to your site. When a web surfer clicks a link from another site to your site, your web stats record the originating site as the referrer. For instance, if you had a link to your site listed on FindAccountants.com, your site stats would show you this site URL and the number of visitors they referred to you. This is extremely useful for determining the efficacy of banner ads and link exchanges as well as finding all the various ways people arrive at your site. You can determine the actual pages that contain links to your web site as well. Some of these will be links you have arranged, and some will be pleasant surprises. By knowing precisely where your visitors are coming from, you are able to tune your promotional efforts and search engine placements to maximize your site's effectiveness.

Top Page URLs: This metric tells you the top pages on your site that were viewed. This is an excellent way to see if the information you want visitors to see is actually being seen.

Status Codes: More a measurement for your designer than for you, this report lets you know how many times pages were unavailable. If you have a lot of pages that show in this report, your designer will need to find where the problems lie and correct them to make the page viewable again.

Web Site Strategies

You'll be able to choose the stats that are most meaningful to you based on the goals for your site. For example, I have a few clients who are not interested in search engine rankings. They do not want to be found on the search engines and spend no time on marketing via the engines. They do care about pointing people to their web site, so they can read about the firm and its services. For these firms, statistics on the length of visit and depth of visit are very important. The fact that they only had a small amount of visitors to the site for the month should not matter because their number one goal is for their visitors to have a deep experience.

These clients will want to focus on stats that tell them how they are doing with their particular goals such as:

- how many pages were viewed
- the most frequent exit page
- the pathway each visitor followed through the site
- and more

With this information, site owners can make adjustments that may affect visitor behavior in how they navigate the site, which pages are viewed and in what order, the length of time spent on the pages and so on.

Here is a huge secret — hardly any service professionals spend much time looking at this information! You can be at the head of the pack simply by reviewing (or having your site designer review) some easy-to-read data each month and making a few simple adjustments in accordance with what you find. Use this information to constantly improve your visitor's experience and your web site, and you will, in turn, constantly improve your bottom line.

To learn more about this topic and stay on top of the latest trends in web analysis, visit www.webanalyticsassociation.com

14

Finding a Web Design Firm

"A thousand mile journey begins with one step."
Lao Tsu
Father of Taoism

Unfortunately, web designers do not need to be licensed to hang up a shingle. As both a web designer and a CPA, I find this very disturbing. I know that, as an accountant, I had to spend four years in college learning about debits and credits and months in the summer studying for the CPA exam. Then I spent two years toiling in public accounting to get my license. As a web designer, all a person has to do is say s/he is one.

Many of the web designers I know have either come from a graphic design background or a programming background. The majority of the graphic designers are very concerned with the look and feel of the site, but have very little interest in the site as a business-generating tool. The sites are beautifully created, but have a lot of graphics without much copy. To me, this is a disservice, as beautiful graphics won't sell your firm to prospective clients. Sites without much copy are also generally shunned by the search engines.

Programmers who become web designers have the opposite tendencies. They really care about the internal coding of the site, but the design may be lacking. Although I said that beautiful graphics won't turn prospects into clients, a poorly designed site will turn that prospect away in a flash. What is best is a good sense of balance: the right amount of graphics and text with a splash of SEO for good measure. How do you find such people?

I recommend the following steps:

1. Create a request for proposal.
2. Compile a list of web designers.
3. Request proposals.
4. Meet with potential web design firms.
5. Evaluate proposals and meet with top candidates.
6. Review references.
7. Make a decision.

Create a Request for Proposal

As a CPA, you are probably very familiar with responding to requests for proposals (RFPs). Now, you get the chance to create your own for a change.

Since you have a spent a lot of time planning the design or redesign of your web site, you have a very clear idea of what role your web site will play. Not to mention, you have all the wonderful worksheets that contain every detail about your site. This is very important to convey to potential web site designers. You should provide your designer with:

- your firm's target market information
- the primary purpose for your web site
- a list of potential pages for your web site
- search engine objectives
- emarketing objectives (ezines, linking, etc.)
- other needs for your site including hosting, domain name registration, etc.
- a time frame
- a budget

In addition, you can also use the RFP included at the end of this chapter.

Compile a List of Web Designers

The first stop should be a search engine. Type in the name of your city or area along with the keyphrase "web design" (not the quotes) and see what local web design firms are on the first two pages. If SEO is important to you, you'll want to work with a company who is listed high in the search engine results. Why? If they can't get their own site ranked highly, how much success do you think they would have with yours? You can also check with area Chambers of Commerce or the Yellow Pages and ask for recommendations from other professional firms. In addition, you can reference other web sites you like. Normally, at the bottom of the home page is a link to the design firm's web site.

Meet with Potential Web Design Firms

After you have come up with your list, send out your RFP with a deadline for reply. Many web development companies require a meeting with prospective clients to discuss the project before returning RFPs. This gives the design firm an opportunity to discuss their ideas or ask questions before obligating themselves to your site. Once this initial conversation happens, the web designer can then come back with an accurate and complete proposal that truly addresses your needs.

Evaluate Proposals and Meet with Top Candidates

Once you get all replies, you can begin to narrow the field. Set up a time to meet with the top three web design companies before making a final decision. Make sure that you fully understand each proposal. Ask for clarification on any items you don't understand. Also, during these interviews, be sure to ask the five suggested questions below.

1. **How do you incorporate search engine techniques when creating web sites?**

   Why You Care: It has recently been reported that only 30% of web sites are listed in the search engines. All web designers state that they care about search engine optimization when creating sites, but few really incorporate the techniques when your site is actually built.

Most Wanted Response: You want your web design firm to tell you they plan to determine keyphrases for your site at the beginning of the project and incorporate them into the title, content and META tags of your site. You also want them to create your site without the use of frames or 100% Flash pages.

Bottom Line: There are other factors (besides web design) that impact search engine optimization, but these design elements will give you a giant boost up with your rankings. Oftentimes, high rankings are as much about what you don't include as what you do include.

2. **What is your turnaround time?**

Why You Care: You'll want your site finished in a reasonable amount of time. Unfortunately, I've come across many businesses that have waited over a year for their site to be completed.

Most Wanted Response: You'll want to hear your web designer offer a specific time frame for site completion. While the web site designer will be dependent upon you for delivery of graphics and content, the designer should be able to discuss a typical schedule and the turnaround time, once you have provided the appropriate materials.

Bottom Line: Don't get stuck for months without a site while you wait for your designer. Make sure you feel comfortable with the designer's response.

3. **Do you use Cascading Style Sheets?**

Why You Care: A cascading style sheet works

behind the scenes to create the look of your entire site. This is preferred to regular HTML formatting for five reasons:

1. Your site loads much faster because file sizes are smaller.

2. Lower maintenance fees. Your designer can update the look of your entire site with one single change to the style sheet.

3. Makes your site more search engine friendly as it reduces the lines of coding.

4. Increases accessibility to your site for visually impaired visitors.

5. It's the wave of the future. Embedded styles on your site could soon be obsolete.

Most Wanted Response: Yes!

Bottom Line: You work hard for your money. Don't waste it on unnecessary maintenance fees or risk having to recreate your site in the next year or two.

4. **Will my site be viewable by all users on all browsers?**

Why You Care: Unfortunately, you cannot control what browser (Internet Explorer, Netscape, Firefox, Mozilla, Opera, Web TV, etc.) a visitor to your site will use. Some sites look great in one browser and horrible in another. A good web designer, however, can make sure your site looks the way it should when viewed in a variety of browsers.

Most Wanted Response: Your designer should use necessary techniques to ensure your site will appear, as it should, in several different browsers. This means your site should actually be viewed in several different browsers as well as several different versions of these browsers. In addition, the site should be checked to ensure that the code is correct. (Dr. HTML and W3C Validator are popular services.)

Bottom Line: Don't push visitors away with a web site that only looks good in one version of Internet Explorer!

5. **How will my business/organization benefit from a web site?**

Why You Care: As you know, web sites can fulfill many different needs for a business or organization. For example, service professionals may want a site to generate qualified leads and help with the processing of client information, etc. You want your designer to understand the benefits of a web site specifically for CPAs and to be able to communicate what s/he feels are the biggest reasons for you to commit to a new web site.

Most Wanted Response: Your designer should explain her/his process to learn about your business and business model so s/he can create a site specifically to meet the needs of your organization.

Bottom Line: Your designer has to fully understand your business, or your site won't function in the capacity you intend for it to function.

Review References

Get references and actually call them. Remember that web designers are not licensed. There are no regulatory agencies that oversee web design. There is no board or government agency that has listings of designers who have done great work or who have had nothing but complaints.

My intent is not to scare you, but to inform you when I say that anyone can call himself or herself a web designer. You want to be sure that these companies have produced the work they claim to have produced and that the clients were (and still are) happy with the results.

Make a Decision

Creating a web site is a major investment, and you'll want to be sure you're working with someone who is as devoted to the success of your site as you are. Finding a good, competent web designer takes effort on your part, but will be well worth the time you spend.

Now that you have all the information in, have met with the designers and have compared their time frames and costs with your own schedule and budget, it's time to decide.

Who wins? Who will be your designer? Call them and let them know. I'm sure they'll be thrilled!

Web Site Request For Proposal Worksheet

This is a Request For Proposal for _____

CPA firm, located at _____

_____.

Your contact for this RFP is _____

S/he may be reached via telephone at (   ) _____

or by email at _____.

Deadline for Reply Is: _____

The web site will include roughly _____ pages including:

_____	_____
_____	_____
_____	_____
_____	_____
_____	_____
_____	_____
_____	_____
_____	_____
_____	_____
_____	_____
_____	_____

Please return your RFP with a minimum of five references, the educational and/or experience history of the designer(s) who will be working on this project, a minimum of three previous sites similar to ours that you have completed and your company history.

Worksheets are also included which detail information on:

- Goals for the site
- Target audience analysis
- Sites we find credible
- Sites for which we like the design

You will also find questionnaires we would like completed and returned containing questions on:

- Copywriting
- Organic Search Engine Optimization
- Pay-Per-Click Campaigns
- Ezine Design

Please also provide the answers to the following questions:

Are graphics an additional cost? _____
If so, what is the fee?_____

Do you offer ezine design? _____ If so, please include the cost in accordance with the attached worksheet.

If needed, do you provide programming services? _____
What is the cost for these services? _____
_____
_____

It is our expectation that ownership of the site, in full, will revert to our firm upon final payment. At this time, all files, passwords, codes, user names, graphics, programming, etc. become the sole property of our organization. Is this your normal policy?

_____

If you need additional space, make copies of this worksheet or use notebook paper.

NOTE: Visit www.KLSWebSolutions.com/Worksheets to print work-sheets from the Internet.

Works Cited

Chapter One

Anklesaria, Nissa et al. "Yahoo! And OMD Reveal Study
Depicting Life Without The Internet."Yahoo!, Inc. Apr 2004.
http://docs.yahoo.com/docs/pr/release1183.html

Lohr, Steven. "Just Googling It Is Striking Fear Into Companies."
New York Times. The New York Times Company. 6 Nov 2005.

Waxman, Sharon. "Cruise's Shift of Publicists Pleases
Hollywood." *New York Times*. The New York Times Company.
9 Nov 2005.

Chapter Three

Google, Inc., www.google.com .

Wikipedia Free Encyclopedia. "Search Engine." *As viewed*
18 Apr 2006. http://en.wikipedia.org/wiki/Search_engine

Elizabeth Brown, CPA, www.elizabethbrowncpa.com

Rainie, Lee and Jeremy Shermak. "Pew Internet & American Life
Project: Search Engine Use."Pew Research Center. Nov 2005.

Chapter Four

Godin, Seth. *Purple Cow*. Portfolio Hardcover. May 2003.

Waugh, Troy. *101 Marketing Strategies for Accounting, Law,
Consulting and Professional Service Firms*. John Wiley & Sons.
12 Apr 2004.

Chapter Five

Kaja Gam Design, www.kajagamdesign.com.

Small Business Administration, www.sba.gov

Weber State University Study as quoted in:
Addams, H. Lon, PhD, and Anthony Allred, PhD, "Why the
Fastest-Growing Companies Hire and Fire Their Auditors."
The CPA Journal. New York State Society of CPAs. May 2002.

Boress, Allan, CPA, CFE and Michael G. Cummings, MBA.
"Mastering the Art of Marketing Professional Services:
A Step-by-Step Best Practices Guide." *A Step-by-Step Best
Practice Guide*. The American Institute of Certified Public
Accountants. 2002.

Chapter Six
Google, Inc., www.google.com.

Koch, Richard. *The 80/20 Principle*. Currency. 19 Oct 1999.

Tischler, Linda. "The Beauty of Simplicity." *Fast Company*.
Nov 2005. p 52.

Chapter Seven
Allegory Floral Design, www.allegoryflowers.com.

Bank of America, www.bankofamerica.com.

CMO Council/KnowledgeStorm 2005 Online Content Survey
Report. 23 Sep 2005. http://au.knowledgestorm.com/ksau/
search/viewabstract/77699/

Cornerstone, www.colorado-retaining-walls.com.

Gladwell, Malcolm. *Blink: The Power of Thinking Without Thinking.* Little, Brown. 11 Jan 2005.

Hoff-Barthelson Music School, www.hbms.org.

Landmark Creations International, www.landmarkcreations.com.

Naturally First, www.naturallyfirst.com.

The Society for Marketing Professional Services, www.smps.org.

Chapter Eight

Cruise Vacation Center, www.cruisevacationcenter.com.

"The Stanford-Poynter Project." *Eyetracking Online News.* Stanford University and The Poynter Institute. 2000. www.poynterextra.org/et/i.htm

"Internet Use Rising Among Developing-Country Firms, But E-Business Lags Behind." United Nations Conference on Trade and Development. Dec 2004. http://www.unctad.org/templates/webflyer.asp?docid=5655&intItemID=1528&lang=1

Wordtracker, www.wordtracker.com.

Chapter Nine

"Eye Tracking Study." Enquiro, EyeTools, and Did It. 2005. http://www.enquiro.com/eyetrackingreport.asp

Greenspan, Robyn. "Jupiter: Online Ad Market to Reach $16.1B." *ClickZ News.* Incisive Interactive Marketing LLC. 27 Jul 2004. www.clickz.com/news/article.php/3386881

Joachims, Thorsten, et al. "Accurately Interpreting Clickthrough Data as Implicit Feedback." Cornell University. 15 Aug 2005. www.cs.cornell.edu/People/tj/publications/joachims_etal_05a.pdf

Moran, Mike and Bill Hunt. *Search Engine Marketing, Inc.: Driving Search Traffic to Your Company's Web Site*. IBM Press. 21 Jul 2005.

Chapter Twelve

Business Know-How. www.BusinessKnowHow.com. ©2005-2006, All Rights Reserved. Reprinted with permission from Business Know-How.

"Email Marketing Metrics Report: H2 2005," MailerMailer LLC. Sep 2005. www.mailermailer.com/metrics/

"End-User Study on Email Hygiene." The Radicati Group, Inc. and Mirapoint, Inc. Apr 2005. http://www.radicati.com/registry.asp?pub=75

Kaja Gam Design, www.kajagamdesign.com.

Index

Services Available

Kristi Stangeland is President of KLS Web Solutions and is also a licensed CPA. Kristi has a multifaceted background in accounting & finance, technology, business strategy and the arts. She uses that knowledge to partner with you in designing the most effective site for your business.

If you would like to contact Kristi about web design for your firm, she can be reached at:

914-478-8480

or at www.KLSWebSolutions.com.